D1322914

Reading Ethnographic Research

ASPECTS OF MODERN SOCIOLOGY

General Editor: Professor Maurice Craft, Foundation Dean of Humanities and Social Science, Hong Kong University of Science and Technology

SOCIAL RESEARCH

Reading Ethnographic Research: A Critical Guide

Martyn Hammersley

LONGMAN
London and New York

Addison Wesley Longman Limited
Edinburgh Gate, Harlow
Essex CM20 2JE, England
and Associated Companies throughout the world.

Published in the United States of America
by Addison Wesley Longman Publishing, New York

First published 1990
Third impression 1996

British Library Cataloguing in Publication Data
Hammersley, Martyn
    Reading ethnographic research. – (Aspects of modern
    sociology, social research).
    1. Ethnography. Research
    I. Title   II. Series
    306.072

ISBN 0–582–05310–2

Library of Congress Cataloguing in Publication Data
Hammersley, Martyn
    1. Communication in ethnology. 2. Ethnology — Authorship.
    1. Ethnology — Study and teaching. I. Title.   II. Series.
    GN307.5.H35 1991
    305.8'0072 — dc20

Set in 10/11 pt. Times Roman
Produced through Longman Malaysia, PA

CONTENTS

EDITOR'S PREFACE

The first series in Longman's *Aspects of Modern Sociology* library was concerned with the social structure of modern Britain, and was intended for students following professional and other courses in universities, polytechnics, colleges of education, and elsewhere in further and higher education, as well as for those members of a wider public wishing to pursue an interest in the nature and structure of British society.

This further series sets out to examine the history, aims, techniques and limitations of social research, and it is hoped that it will be of interest to the same readership. It will seek to offer an informative but not uncritical introduction to some of the methodologies of social science.

Maurice Craft

To Joan, Rachel and Paul, again!

A U T H O R ' S   P R E F A C E

There is now a considerable literature about ethnographic or qualitative methodology, including many texts for students. However, this literature concentrates very largely on how to *do* ethnographic research. Very little attention has been given to how we should *read and assess* ethnographic studies. And yet this is an important, and by no means straightforward, task.

Of course, we tend to treat reading as a relatively unproblematic skill that most of us learn when we are children. We talk of 'learning to read' as if it were something that has a well-defined end; but in a sense we are always (or should always be) still learning how to read. A little reflection reveals that reading implies understanding; and that the process of understanding texts is a complex matter that is closely bound up with the nature of the ideas that writers seek to communicate, and with our own background knowledge. Not only are there texts whose vocabulary we may not comprehend, those that rely on esoteric mathematical symbols or that are written in unfamiliar natural languages for example; but even when we understand the grammar and vocabulary we may not always understand the message intended. A mundane example of such lack of understanding happened to me recently. When visiting friends, the son of the house (who was cooking the evening meal) said: 'Tell my mother she looks like a vegetable.' I understood the meaning of the words, but I could not understand the purpose (and therefore the meaning) of the message. It only made sense when I discovered later that his mother had told him that if he cooked her any more vegetarian meals she would look like a vegetable!' This illustrates that the meaning of what people say and write is not given merely by the meanings of the words used, it also depends on the context in which communication occurs and the motivation for the message built into that context. Furthermore, context is almost endlessly extendable. At the extreme it may involve taking account of the wider society in which the communication occurs and even the history of that society. Finally, we must remember that we read not just to understand, but to learn and use. At one level this may be a matter of deriving information from what we read, and implicit in this is the assessment of the validity and value of that information. Equally, though, what we read may stimulate lines of thinking that owe more to our own concerns and knowledge than to the message of the text.

The complexity and importance of reading has long been recognised in the humanities. From at least the time of the Renaissance there has been a concern with how to understand texts produced in earlier periods, especially the writings of the Ancient Greeks and Romans, and of course the Bible. The Renaissance Humanists were aware of the cultural differences between the societies from which these texts came and their own; and the problems of understanding that this could cause. In the Anglo-American world much of this interest in understanding texts has come to be concentrated in the discipline of literary criticism. Early in this century the influence of what was labelled the 'new criticism', especially the work of I. A. Richards, placed great emphasis on reading. One of Richards' books is entitled *How to Read a Page*, and it remains instructive today (Richards, 1943). There have been many changes in literary studies since the time of Richards, but if anything there is now even greater emphasis on the active, critical and creative character of reading.[1]

Reading is not a simple matter, then. And in the case of ethnographic research reports this is a particularly important point. The style in which these are written is to a large extent non-technical: it is modelled on stylistic forms that we are familiar with in everyday life, such as those found in travel writing, newspaper articles and even novels. It may be concluded from this that such reports are straightforwardly readable by anyone. Indeed, ethnographers sometimes claim this to be one of the great virtues of their accounts in comparison with reports based on quantitative analysis. This is deceptive, however. As we shall see, in some ways the familiar character of ethnographic writing makes it more difficult to read and assess properly. A colleague of mine once formulated a tentative law about the ethnographer's task of gaining access to settings in order to study them. Atkinson's hypothesis states that the easier it is to gain access, the more troublesome life in the field will be for the ethnographer (Atkinson, 1981b). It seems to me that something analogous may apply to research texts: the more immediately accessible they seem, the more difficult they may be to read and assess. This is intended as no more than a warning: that apparently easily understandable texts can turn out to have meanings that are elusive.

The form that reading takes depends in part on our purposes. When reading for entertainment we are likely to adopt a different mode than when we study a text in order to learn from it. Furthermore, we may adopt different approaches depending on the character or detail of understanding we require. My concern in this book is with reading ethnographic studies for the purpose of coming to reasonable judgements about the general value of the claims they make. This is the sort of reading and assessment that is (or ought to be) characteristic of the way researchers review one another's work, in private and in public; as well as that appropriate for students working on literature relevant to their courses and projects. There are other ways of approaching ethnographic texts, however: in terms of the linguistic and rhetorical resources they employ; or with an interest in how they came to be written, what they signify about the context that produced them, etc. Such things may be of relevance in the kind of reading I am concerned with here, but only as background. Equally, ethnographic research may be assessed for how well it helps us solve practical problems, or for what it can tell us about the competence of the researcher and/or about the effectiveness or ethical status of the research strategies employed. What I am concerned with in this book is an essential element of such assessments, but it is not sufficient.[2]

Reading plays an important (and rather neglected) role in science and scholarship. These are collective enterprises and the work of any individual researcher needs to be coordinated with that of others. More than this, though, the intellectual authority of scholarship and science depends on the communal assessment of its products. It is only because scientific claims are (or are assumed to be) subjected to systematic and rigorous assessment by fellow scientists that we tend to treat them (other things being equal) as more reliable than the views of non-scientists; and, of course, our confidence is not always justified. Even in the case of the natural sciences, this process of monitoring and communal assessment cannot guarantee the validity of the results. For a variety of reasons, the process is somewhat less effective in the social sciences (including ethnography). One of my hopes is that this book may encourage more, and more effective, assessment of ethnographic studies. It has often struck me that the amount of time and care spent producing ethnographic accounts is probably not balanced by sufficient attention to the understanding and assessment of those accounts on the part of readers. Certainly, the amount of space given in journals and books to the presentation of the findings of new research is rather greater than that devoted to the detailed assessment of such work by others.[3]

For students on social science courses, the reading of ethnographic and other kinds of studies is essential and inescapable. But, as I noted earlier, very often little guidance is given about how to do this. It is the purpose of this book to provide such guidance, based on my own experience both of doing ethnographic research and of reading it. I am convinced that we can learn from one another's experience, in this area as in others. That said, I must emphasise the limits of what can be offered by this book. First, it is not based on a consensus among ethnographers about how to approach reading their work. As we shall see, there is considerable disagreement about the nature of ethnography, and relatively little attention has been given to the criteria by which it should be assessed. Second, what is presented here is not a set of steps which (if followed) will guarantee 'good reading'. No formulae of this kind are available. Third, what I have to say is limited to only one part of the process of understanding: the identification and assessment of the claims and conclusions presented by the author. I do not, and do not believe that I can, deal with the more creative and reflective levels of reading. But the latter may be more fruitful if based on sound understanding and assessment of the more mundane kind that I am concerned with here.[4]

What I provide in this book, then, is a framework of ideas for thinking about and approaching the reading and assessment of ethnographic texts. It is not offered as the only way that this can be done; though it is the best that I can give at the moment. Many ethnographers will not like one or other aspect of what I recommend (and some may not like any of it!). So, as reader of this text, you may well question what I have written here. That is all to the good. I hope that your reading of this book will be as reflective and critical as the sort of reading of ethnographic texts that I advocate.

OUTLINE OF THE BOOK

The first chapter provides a sketch of ethnography and of recent developments in methodological thinking about it. I emphasise the diverse and ill-defined nature of the ethnographic tradition, and look at some of the key debates about its scientific status. Chapter 2 is concerned with the process of understanding ethnographic texts in the narrow sense of identifying what the author was seeking to communicate and why. Clearly, such understanding is an essential preliminary to any assessment of the claims and conclusions of a study. An overview of what is involved in assessing ethnographic texts is provided in Chapter 3. Of special importance here is the question of the criteria by which ethnographic studies should be judged. This question raises some fundamental issues about the nature of ethnographic research. The next two chapters, 4 and 5, discuss what I take to be the two main assessment criteria that should be applied to ethnographic studies: validity and relevance. In Chapter 6 I illustrate the approach to understanding and assessment that I have advocated by applying it to an example of my own work. Finally, Chapter 7 widens the focus, locating in a broader context the sort of assessment with which I have been primarily concerned.

NOTES

1. For accounts of more recent approaches to literary criticism, see Norris (1982) and Eagleton (1983).
2. These other forms of assessment are not my main concern, but I shall discuss some of them briefly in the final chapter.
3. In this respect those in the survey and experimental research traditions may be somewhat in advance of ethnographers. See, for example, the following detailed assessments of major survey research and experimental projects: Merton and Lazarsfeld (1950); Christie and Jahoda (1954); McKinney (1973); and Miller (1986). There is much reviewing of ethnographic studies, of course; but often the reviews are brief and superficial. The following are, however, examples of more extended assessments of particular ethnographic studies: Blumer (1939); D.H. Hargreaves (1978); Freeman (1984); Foster (1990); Hammersley (1990a and b).
4. There are no other books dealing specifically with the reading and assessment of ethnographic research, as far as I am aware. However, in advocating the synthesis of ethnographic studies Noblitt and Hare (1988) cover some of the same ground, but from a very different perspective to that adopted in this book. There are a few books that deal with the assessment of social research in general: for example, Tripodi *et al.* (1969), Katzer *et al.* (1978), Stern (1979), and Rose (1982). In general these adopt a fairly traditional approach based on the quantitative model, but Rose does give some separate discussion to qualitative research.

ACKNOWLEDGEMENTS

The work on which this book is based has been carried out over a considerable period of time, and I am grateful to many colleagues for their assistance, witting and unwitting: especially, Stephen Ball, Barry Cooper, Jeff Evans, Peter Foster, Roger Gomm, Andy Hargreaves, Donald Mackinnon, John Scarth, Thomas Schwandt, John K. Smith and Peter Woods. As usual, my family bore some of the burden of this work, for which I thank them.

PUBLISHER'S ACKNOWLEDGEMENTS

We are grateful to the following for permission to reproduce copyright material;

Basil Blackwell Ltd for an extract and for fig. 1 which has been adapted from a table from *Receiving Juvenile Justice* by H Parker et al (pub 1981); Columbia University Press for an extract & abridged extracts from *Soulside* by U Hannerz (pub 1969); International Thomson Publishing Services Ltd for an abridged extract from *The Ceremonial Order of the Clinic* by P Strong (pub Routledge, 1979); Open University Press for the Chapter 'Staffroom News' by Martyn Hammersley from *Classrooms & Staffrooms* edited by A Hargreaves & P Woods (pub 1984). Andrew Pollard for table 1 from 'Coping Strategies and the Multiplication of Differentiation', in the *British Educational Research Journal*; Routledge and Kegan Paul for fig. 2 from *Social Relations in the Secondary School* by David Hargreaves.

CHAPTER 1

Introduction: the nature of ethnography

The term 'ethnography' is not clearly defined in common usage, and there is some disagreement about what count and do not count as examples of it. Furthermore, the meaning of the term overlaps with that of several others – such as 'qualitative method', 'interpretative research', 'case study', 'participant observation', 'life history method', 'ethogenics', etc.; and these terms are not used in very precisely defined ways either.[1] This diversity and looseness of terminology reflects some dissensus even on fundamental issues among advocates of these approaches. More than this, though, it results from a certain vagueness in thinking about methodological issues that arises from a widespread emphasis among ethnographers on the primacy of research practice over 'theory' about how to do it. Sometimes this amounts to an anti-methodological and anti-theoretical prejudice. Ethnographers tend to distrust general formulations, whether about human social life or about how to do research, in favour of a concern with particulars. But however much one distrusts philosophy, one cannot escape it. As we shall see, the practice of ethnography is surrounded by a host of philosophical ideas. And while we must recognise the limits of abstract reasoning, we should press it as far as it will go in seeking to provide a sound basis, whether for doing research or for reading and assessing its products.

I shall examine some of the philosophical ideas associated with ethnography later in this chapter. First, though, I want to look briefly at the forms of research design, data collection and analysis that are characteristic of ethnography (defined in a broad sense), and to sketch something of ethnography's history.

ETHNOGRAPHY AS METHOD

In terms of method, generally speaking, the term 'ethnography' refers to social research that has most of the following features:

(a) People's behaviour is studied in everyday contexts, rather than under experimental conditions created by the researcher.

(b) Data are gathered from a *range* of sources, but observation and/or relatively informal conversations are usually the main ones.

(c) The approach to data collection is 'unstructured' in the sense that it does not involve following through a detailed plan set up at the beginning; nor are the categories used for interpreting what people say and do pre-given or fixed. This does not mean that the research is unsystematic; simply that initially the data are collected in as raw a form, and on as wide a front, as feasible.

(d) The focus is usually a single setting or group, of relatively small scale. In life history research the focus may even be a single individual.

(e) The analysis of the data involves interpretation of the meanings and functions of human actions and mainly takes the form of verbal descriptions and explanations, with quantification and statistical analysis playing a subordinate role at most.

As a set of methods, ethnography is not far removed from the sort of approach that we all use in everyday life to make sense of our surroundings. It is less specialised and less technically sophisticated than approaches like the experiment or the social survey; though all social research methods have their historical origins in the ways in which human beings gain information about their world in everyday life. The more specific origins of ethnography lie in the writings of travellers concerned to inform their fellows about other societies, whether it is Herodotus exploring the western provinces of the Persian Empire (Rowe, 1965) or Hans Stade reporting on his captivity by the 'wild tribes of Eastern Brazil' (Pratt, 1986). These other societies were not always geographically distant either: thus, in the nineteenth century we have Friedrich Engels, the son of a German industrialist, investigating the lives of Lancashire factory workers; Tocqueville reporting on *Democracy in America*; and Henry Mayhew writing newspaper articles about the working-class underlife of London (Engels, 1892; Tocqueville, 1966; Mayhew, 1861–2 and 1971).

The writings of such people form the early history of what we would today call social or cultural anthropology and sociology.[2] However, the data on which these reports were based were often unsystematic and sometimes misleading; and the analysis was frequently speculative and evaluative (though sometimes valuable for all that). One of the most important features of the development of the social science disciplines in the nineteenth and early twentieth centuries was the attempt to overcome such deficiencies of earlier accounts. The influence of the natural sciences was particularly important here. Even in the nineteenth century many anthropologists relied on the reports of travellers and missionaries for their data, but from the turn of the century it became widely accepted that it was necessary for them to collect their own data, and to do so in a systematic and rigorous manner. Initially, this tended to take the form of expeditions that were primarily concerned with collecting artifacts, both material and non-material (such as myths). Later, particularly through the influence of Bronislaw Malinowski, it came to be required that the anthropologist live among the people being studied, learn their language, and observe their lives first hand.[3] In addition, anthropologists became much more concerned with avoiding the speculative excesses of their predecessors and with adopting a scientific approach to the handling of evidence. Since the early decades of the century, ethnography has been the staple research method employed by social and cultural anthropologists, though they have sometimes combined it with social survey work and even with the use of psychological tests.

Sociologists have also employed ethnographic methods since early in the present century, though it has not occupied as central a place in their discipline as in anthropology. One of the earliest developments here arose in what is sometimes referred to as the 'Chicago School of Sociology'. Chicago was among the first universities in the United States to establish a sociology department, and that department was very influential in the 1920s and 1930s. Sociologists working there became increasingly preoccupied with the character of their city. It had experienced a tremendous growth in size in the twenty years each side of the turn of the century, and many of the new inhabitants were European immigrants. Given this, Chicago sociologists came to see the city as a kind of natural laboratory in which the diversity and processes of change characteristic of human behaviour could be studied. While investigation of the city had begun before his arrival, Robert Park, an ex-newspaper reporter, was the main force behind the series of studies produced by students at Chicago in the 1920s, 1930s and 1940s. Some of the work carried out was statistical in character, but much of it took the form of what was then called 'case study research'. This involved detailed investigation of a single case, or a small number of cases, these being areas of the city (as with Zorbaugh's exploration of the different parts of North Side Chicago and their inhabitants), (Zorbaugh, 1929), city organisations (for example, Cressey's study of the taxi-dance halls where men paid the dancers a fare for each dance), (Cressey, 1932), or even individual people (as in the case of Shaw's *The Jack Roller*, a life history of what we would now refer to as a 'mugger') (Shaw, 1930). These studies used methods that approximated the ethnography of today, though they tended to place greater emphasis on written documents.[4]

At around the same time as the Chicagoans were engaged in studying their city, another important source of ethnographic method in sociology and anthropology was emerging: what came to be called the 'community study'. The inspiration for this was in large part the application of anthropological methods to the study of Western societies. One of the first and most important community studies was the investigation of 'Middletown' (the small town of Muncie, Indiana) by Robert and Helen Lynd. On the basis of participation and observation in the community and interviews with community members, they described key aspects of life in Middletown: 'getting a living', 'making a home', 'training the young', 'using leisure', 'engaging in religious practices' and 'engaging in community activities'. This specification of aspects of community life derived from a scheme developed by anthropologists for studying non-Western societies. The Lynds had originally been concerned with religious beliefs and practices, but they realised that these could only be understood in the context of community life as a whole (Lynd and Lynd 1929). Following this, many other communities, usually but not always small towns, were studied; and sometimes they were restudied. The Lynds themselves returned to Middletown some ten years after their first investigation to document the changes that had occurred, and especially the effects of the Depression (Lynd and Lynd, 1937). Later, a similar tradition of studying small communities was established in Britain, producing, for example, Williams' study of the village of Gosforth (Williams, 1956), Emmett's account of Llanfrothen (Emmett, 1964) and Stacey's study and restudy of Banbury (Stacey, 1960; Stacey *et al.*, 1975). In addition, a number of investigations were mounted by the Institute for Community Study in the 1950s and 1960s, most notably of working-class areas in London (see Platt, 1971). This community study tradition has witnessed a decline in the past twenty years in both the United States and Britain; though there are signs of a British revival among anthropologists (Cohen, 1982 and 1986).[5]

As I noted, a crucial element of the emergence of specialised social sciences was the drive to make them systematic and rigorous, on the model of natural science. However, this took a variety of forms, depending on what were believed to be the essential features of science, and ideas about the extent to which and ways in which human social life differed from the subject matter of the physical sciences. Within anthropology, it resulted in an emphasis on more direct observation by the anthropologist and the attempt to make the descriptions produced as objective as possible, being neither deceived by the historical myths of the natives nor blinded by one's own cultural assumptions and prejudices. An analogous emphasis on documented and first-hand information was the initial effect of the drive for scientific status in sociology, as represented by the early Chicago School. From at least the 1930s onward, though, at Chicago and elsewhere in the United States, social *science* came to be associated with the statistical method. By the 1940s and 1950s survey research was the dominant method within US sociology. This is not to suggest that case study and community study work ceased. Research in anthropology continued much as before. Even in sociology, ethnographic studies still appeared, notably William Foote Whyte's

Streetcorner Society (an investigation of the cultures to be found among young males in an Italian-American community), and the work of Everett Hughes and his students on various occupations, and on medical and educational institutions. In addition, partly stemming from the dominance of quantitative method, there were increasing efforts to enhance the rigour of ethnographic research.[6]

However, in the 1960s the overwhelming dominance of survey methodology in US sociology and elsewhere started to wane, and ethnographic research became more widely advocated and practised (though survey research has remained very influential in the United States, more so than in Britain). The growth in ethnography was especially notable in the study of deviant groups, but also in the sociology of medicine and other areas. In Britain there was a relatively sudden increase of interest in ethnographic research towards the end of the 1960s, largely as a result of the diversification of theoretical approaches to include symbolic interactionism, phenomenology and ethnomethodology. A considerable body of British ethnographic research has been produced since then; here again notably in the sociologies of deviance and medicine, but also in the field of education.[7]

The resurgence of interest in ethnography within sociology in the 1960s, 1970s and 1980s – following a period in which survey research had become almost identified with sociological method – was accompanied by considerable debate about methodological issues. This occurred not just between advocates of survey and ethnographic research but also among ethnographers themselves. In the next section I want to look briefly at these debates.

METHODOLOGICAL DEBATES ABOUT ETHNOGRAPHY

Debates about ethnography can be broadly divided into two categories, with the first preoccupying discussions in the 1960s and 1970s, the second becoming more salient in the 1980s:

1. Debates centring on criticisms of ethnography for not meeting the criteria assumed by quantitative researchers to be characteristic of science.
2. Arguments that ethnography has not broken sharply enough with, or moved far enough away from, quantitative research and the model of natural science.

I shall look at each of these two sorts of debate in turn.

Criticisms of ethnography for not being 'scientific'

Competition with quantitative approaches to sociology, and especially with survey research, has long shaped the way in which ethnographers have thought about their work, raising the question: Is ethnography scientific? By the 1960s quantitative research in the form of experimentalism and social surveys had become highly developed, and sophisticated methodological literatures had grown up around them which took it for granted that they were implementing scientific method. While there was dissensus about some points, there was considerable agreement on the basics; and in large part this was framed in terms of the positivist outlook that had dominated the philosophy of science in the 1940s and 1950s. Central here was the idea that what was required in empirical research was clear and operational specification of hypotheses; the selection of a research design that allowed those hypotheses to be tested, either by the physical manipulation of variables (as in experiments) or through statistical analysis of large samples of cases (as in survey research); along with the assessment of measurement error by means of reliability (and, more rarely, validity) tests.

Ethnographers responded in several ways to this influential view of the nature of social science methodology:

i)   Some claimed that ethnography is *more* scientific (that is, closer in character to natural science) than quantitative research. In the early decades of the century this was argued on the grounds that case study can produce universal laws not just the probabilistic findings characteristic of statistical method (Znaniecki, 1934). This argument is rarely used today, both because of the statistical character of some parts of more recent work in physics (notably quantum theory), and because most ethnographers have lost faith in the possibility of discovering sociological laws. In recent times, it is more common to find the scientific character of ethnography being justified on the grounds that it is more suited than are experimental and survey research to the nature of human behaviour, in particular to its processual and meaning-laden character (Bruyn, 1966; Blumer, 1969; Harré and Secord, 1973).

ii) A second sort of response involves broadly accepting the view of sociological method characteristic of quantitative research, but treating ethnography as distinctive in its suitability to particular phases of the research process or to particular research problems. For example, it might be regarded as especially appropriate in the pilot stages of social surveys, or the debriefing phases of experiments; and/or it might be seen as well-suited to the study of deviant groups, whose small size and secrecy make them inaccessible to survey research. On this view ethnography may be usefully combined with other methods, which are assumed to have complementary strengths and weaknesses.

iii) A third position is that ethnography represents a different kind of science to that characteristic of the natural sciences. Here quantitative methods may be criticised for aping the natural sciences. Often associated with this is the claim that ethnography is idiographic rather than nomothetic (that it focuses on the unique as much as the general), and/or interpretative rather than observational (that the understanding of human behaviour always involves interpretation not mere physical description).

In their methodological writings ethnographers often combine two or more of these three positions. The first and third are the most common, however, with ethnography viewed as based on assumptions about human society and how it can be best understood that diverge from those implicit in most quantitative research. These assumptions may also be found in milder versions among advocates of the second position. They can be summarised under the headings of naturalism, understanding and discovery:

1. *Naturalism.* This is the view that the aim of social research is to capture the character of naturally occurring human behaviour, and that this can only be achieved by first-hand contact with it, not by inferences from what people do in artificial settings like experiments or from what they say in interviews about what they do elsewhere. This is the reason that ethnographers carry out their research in 'natural' settings, settings that exist independently of the research process, rather than in those set up specifically for the purposes of research. Another important implication of naturalism is that in studying natural settings the researcher should seek to minimise her or his effects on the behaviour of the people being studied. The aim of this is to increase the chances that what is discovered in the setting will be generalisable to other similar settings that have not been researched. Finally, the notion of naturalism implies that social events and processes must be explained in terms of their relationship to the context in which they occur. What is involved here is an appeal to what is sometimes called the 'pattern model of explanation' as against the covering law model characteristic of positivist philosophy of science.[8]

2. *Understanding.* Central here is the argument that human actions differ from the behaviour of physical objects, and even from that of other animals: they do not consist simply of fixed responses or even of learned responses to stimuli, but involve *interpretation* of stimuli and the *construction* of responses. Sometimes this argument reflects a complete rejection of the concept of causality as inapplicable to the social world, and an insistence on the freely constructed character of human actions and institutions. Others argue that causal relations *are* to be found in the social world, but that they differ from the 'mechanical' causality typical of physical phenomena. From this point of view, if we are to be able to explain human actions effectively we must gain an understanding

of the cultural perspectives on which they are based. That this is necessary is obvious when we are studying a society that is alien to us, since we shall find much of what we see and hear puzzling. However, ethnographers argue that it is just as important when we are studying more familiar settings. Indeed, when a setting is familiar the danger of misunderstanding is especially great. It is argued that we cannot assume that we already know others' perspectives, even in our own society, because particular groups and individuals develop distinctive worldviews. This is especially true in large complex societies. Ethnic, occupational, and small informal groups (even individual families or school classes) develop distinctive ways of orienting to the world that may need to be understood if their behaviour is to be explained. Ethnographers argue, then, that it is necessary to learn the culture of the group one is studying before one can produce valid explanations for the behaviour of its members. This is the reason for the centrality of participant observation and unstructured interviewing to ethnographic method.[9]

3. *Discovery.* Another feature of ethnographic thinking is a conception of the research process as inductive or discovery-based; rather than as being limited to the testing of explicit hypotheses. It is argued that if one approaches a phenomenon with a set of hypotheses one may fail to discover the true nature of that phenomenon, being blinded by the assumptions built into the hypotheses. Instead, one should begin research with minimal assumptions so as to maximise one's capacity for learning. It is for this reason that ethnographers rarely begin their research with specific hypotheses. Rather, they have a general interest in some types of social phenomena and/or in some theoretical issue or practical problem. The focus of the research is narrowed and sharpened, and perhaps even changed substantially, as it proceeds. Similarly, and in parallel, theoretical ideas that frame descriptions and explanations of what is observed are developed over the course of the research. Such ideas are regarded as a valuable outcome of, not a precondition for, research.

These methodological principles are closely related, indeed they overlap; and, as I have indicated, they provide the rationale for the specific features of ethnographic method that I outlined earlier. They are also the basis for much ethnographic criticism of quantitative research for failing to capture the true nature of human social behaviour: because it relies on the study of artificial settings and/or on what people say rather than what they do; because it seeks to reduce meanings to what is 'observable'; and because it reifies social phenomena by treating them as more clearly defined and static than they are, and as mechanical products of social and psychological factors.

In turn, of course, quantitative researchers have questioned the scientific status of ethnography. Let us look briefly at the sort of debate there has been on this issue. Here are some of the criticisms that have been made of ethnographic research, along with the sort of answers given to them by ethnographers.[10]

Criticism: Ethnographic research suffers from a lack of precision as a result of the absence of quantification. For example, words like 'often' and 'frequently' are used instead of more precise numerical specifications. In this way it is impressionistic.

Answer: There is nothing intrinsic to ethnography which rejects quantification, and indeed ethnographic studies do sometimes employ it. However, precision is not always important. Where differences are large and obvious it may be that they can be reported in relatively imprecise ways without loss. Furthermore, there is the danger of overprecision: by insisting on precise quantitative measures we may produce figures that are more precise than we can justify given the nature of the data available, and which are therefore misleading.

Criticism: Ethnographic observation and interviewing are subjective in the sense that they are not guided by a structure (in the form of a questionnaire or observational schedule) that would maximise the chances that another observer or interviewer would produce the same data. As a result, ethnographic data are peculiarly subject to bias.

Answer: It is true that in ethnographic research what data are collected depends on the researcher, and to one degree or another reflects her or his personal characteristics. But all knowledge is personal and cultural in some sense. At the same time, ethnographers use techniques designed to ensure that their findings are not idiosyncratic – for example, by comparing data from different sources, a technique sometimes referred to as 'triangulation'. Conversely, the structuring of data that quantitative research employs to overcome subjectivity has reactive effects. In other words, people react to the structure itself, thereby increasing the chances that the behaviour studied is an artifact of the research process and not representative of the phenomena purportedly being studied. Even apart from this, the use of schedules does not solve the problem of subjectivity because the same structure can be interpreted differently by different people. For example, the same question asked by an interviewer at the same point in an interview may mean different things to different people.

Criticism: By studying very small samples ethnographers produce findings that are of little value because they are not generalisable.

Answer: The choice of small samples represents a trade-off between studying cases in depth or in breadth. Ethnography usually sacrifices the latter for the former; survey research does the reverse. And in sacrificing depth, survey researchers both lose relevant information and run the risk of misunderstanding key features of the cases they study. Moreover, one can make claims about the representativeness of findings without relying on statistical sampling, for example by comparing the features of the case studied with aggregate data about the population. Equally, one may study a small selection of cases that are designed to represent key dimensions in terms of which the population is assumed to be structured. (It is worth pointing out that social surveys rarely employ pure random sampling, they too rely on assumptions about the 'stratification' of the population.) Furthermore, ethnographers are often not concerned with empirical generalisation but rather with making theoretical inferences, and this does not require the case studied to be representative.

Criticism: By studying natural settings and only small samples ethnographers rule out the possibility of physical or statistical control of variables, and as a result they are not able to identify causal relationships.

Answer: Even if they exist in the social world, causal relationships are not of the same kind as those to be found in the physical world. Thus, they are not accessible to techniques modelled on investigations in physics. By documenting processes occurring over time and/or by means of comparative analysis of cases, ethnography is able to trace patterns of relationships among social phenomena in their natural context in a way that neither experiments nor social surveys can do.

Criticism: A key feature of science is the possibility of replication, of other scientists checking the findings of an experiment by repeating it. Since ethnography does not follow a well-designed and explicit procedure that is replicable, its findings cannot be checked by others and are therefore unscientific.

Answer: Replication is not always possible in natural science, and it is not always carried out even when it is possible. This indicates that replication is not the only means by which scientists assess one another's work, and is therefore not an essential feature of science. The fact that it may not be possible in ethnography does not therefore detract from the validity of ethnographic findings.

Such debate, not always so politely expressed, has gone on for many years; but in some fields in recent times it has largely subsided in favour of a spirit of detente (Rist, 1977; Smith and Heshusius, 1986). One reason is probably that each side has become much more heterogeneous, so that other targets for criticism and issues for debate have emerged. Since the 1960s and 1970s, though, when debate about the scientific status of ethnography was at its height in British sociology, there has been a trend towards increased adoption of qualitative method.

Much of the methodological thinking of ethnographers, then, has been shaped by a concern to place their work in relation to natural science and quantitative method. This has often involved attempts to draw a sharp line between ethnography on the one hand and journalism and fiction on the other, despite (or perhaps because of!) the similarities. In recent years, however, there has been a noticeable downplaying, if not rejection, of the scientific model among some ethnographers and increased emphasis on the parallels with literature. This probably reflects the growth of questioning about the nature and value of science on the one hand, and the rise of interest in literary theory on the other. It has led to criticism of ethnographic work, from inside and outside, for not making a sharp enough break with the model of natural science and with quantitative method.

Criticisms of ethnography for being too 'scientific'

Until the middle of this century, nineteenth-century confidence in scientific method as *the* source of knowledge remained predominant. But, partly as a result of major reconstructions in physics and the demonstration of its terrible potential for destruction, this confidence began to be undermined. The philosophy of science in the 1950s experienced the collapse of what had previously been a substantial consensus about the nature of science, founded on logical positivism: that it involved the induction of knowledge from a base of observations that were themselves certain, the process of induction transmitting certainty to the knowledge produced. Doubts about the idea of observational certainties and of the possibility of logical induction were not new, but they and their implications came to be taken much more seriously.

Growing doubts about the nature of scientific methodology were symbolised by the impact of Thomas Kuhn's book *The Structure of Scientific Revolutions*, first published in 1962 (Kuhn, 1970). Kuhn argued against views of the history of natural science that portrayed it as a process of cumulative development, achieved by rational investigation founded on evidence. He showed that the work of the scientists involved in many of the major developments of scientific knowledge of the past was shaped by theoretical assumptions about the world that were not themselves based on empirical research; and many of which are now judged to be false. Kuhn further claimed that the history of science, rather than displaying the gradual build-up of knowledge, is punctuated by periods of revolution when the theoretical assumptions underlying the 'paradigm' in terms of which scientists in a particular field have previously operated are challenged and replaced. (An example is the shift from Newtonian physics to relativity and quantum theory in the early part of the twentieth century.) The replacement of one paradigm by another, according to Kuhn, does not occur on the basis simply of rational assessment of evidence. Paradigms are incommensurable: they picture the world in incompatible ways, so that data themselves are interpreted differently by those working within different paradigms. Paradigm shifts occur more through representatives of the old paradigm retiring or dying and those of the new one replacing them than by rational persuasion.[11]

Others have taken these ideas further, for example rejecting the notion of scientific method and the claims of science to produce knowledge (even of the physical world) that is superior to that from other sources, such as religious views (see Feyerabend, 1975 and 1978). And today there remains considerable dissensus among philosophers of science; with disagreement, for example, about whether science provides knowledge of an independent reality or simply a record of successful predictions of experience.[12] None of the various attempts to provide an alternative basis for the claim that science is the distinctive source of soundly based knowledge has created a new consensus. One of the effects of this has been to undermine the capacity of natural science to offer a clear model for the social sciences. At the same time, the horrifying capability of science to produce weapons that maim and kill and industries that destroy the environment has challenged the idea that science represents the spearhead of human progress. And some commentators have sought to argue that the bitter fruits of scientific work indicate the poisonous nature of the plant.[13]

In this new climate, criticism of conventional ethnography has taken a variety of forms. One target has been the separation of research from practice that it inherits from the scientific model, a criticism reflecting an increased concern with the practical value and consequences of knowledge. Critical theory has been particularly important here, advancing as an alternative what I shall call the 'emancipatory' model. Critical theory's view of the nature and role of the social sciences derived from the work of the Frankfurt School of Marxism. Jurgen Habermas is the most influential exponent of this perspective.[14] He argues that the cognitive interest motivating natural science is that of instrumental control; and that while this is legitimate in the investigation of physical phenomena, it is inappropriate for the study of human behaviour. He claims that this instrumental interest lies behind quantitative social science, and criticises it for this reason. Habermas regards interpretative research as more appropriate in social science, and believes it to be founded on a concern with overcoming inter-cultural misunderstanding. However, he argues that even this approach is inadequate in the study of advanced capitalist societies because it fails to address the need to emancipate people from ideology, one element of which is the overextension of ideas about knowledge and reality deriving from the natural sciences to our understanding of human social life.

From this perspective, conventional ethnography may be criticised for simply representing things as they are; or, perhaps even worse, representing them as they *appear* to the people studied. There are two arguments involved here: that ethnography only captures surface appearances not the underlying reality; and that it is concerned only with documenting how things *are*, not with discovering how they might be *changed* for the better. Critical theory, by contrast, is concerned with dispelling ideology and thereby promoting emancipation.

A related development has been the tremendous growth in the influence of feminism, and in particular the attempt to identify aspects of Western thinking, including philosophy and methodology, that betray masculinist bias. The model of the natural sciences and the use of quantitative method have sometimes been criticised as representing such a bias (Graham, 1983). There is considerable diversity in feminist thinking about methodology, but an important theme has been criticism of conventional ethnographic work on similar grounds to critical theorists: that it has been content with mere description rather than being directed towards bringing about emancipation, in this case of women.[15]

An area of special concern to feminists, and to others as well, has been the relationship between researcher and researched, viewed as an aspect of the politics of social research. It has been argued that in more traditional forms of ethnography, as in experimental and survey research, a power relationship is involved. The research is very often focused on relatively powerless groups with the researcher exploiting their powerlessness to carry out the research. Moreover, it is claimed, the research often serves the powerful, perhaps enabling them to exercise more effective control. From this perspective research itself may be a form of domination.[16] Even where researcher and researched are social equals, power is still involved because it is the researcher who makes the decisions about what is to be studied, how, for what purpose, etc. It is argued that not only is this unacceptable in itself, but it distorts the knowledge produced: the findings are often irrelevant to the people being studied, since they are geared to problems defined by social science disciplines and not to those that face the people themselves. Furthermore, research reports are written in language that is not comprehensible to those studied. And such research is often invalid because the ethnographer remains an outsider and fails truly to understand the world from a participant point of view.

Such arguments have been developed in several fields. They are to be found not only among feminists, but also among anthropologists concerned with the role of that discipline in international imperialism, in the field of ethnic relations where the study of ethnic minorities by members of ethnic majorities has been challenged, and also in educational research with the advocacy of 'the teacher as researcher'.

The remedy advocated is participatory research, research by and for participants, with professional researchers playing no more than a facilitative role.[17]

Another way in which the relevance of the scientific model to ethnography has been challenged focuses on ethnographers' claims that their accounts represent reality. As we saw, a central element of the rationale for ethnography has often been that it can capture the nature of human social life more accurately than quantitative methods. This is a key element of the ethnographic commitment to both 'naturalism' and 'discovery'. However, some critics (including some ethnographers) argue that any such appeal to the representation of reality is ill-founded. Such questioning of the representational capacity of ethnography can arise simply from applying the concept of understanding to the research process itself. If it is true that people construct interpretations of the world, and that different groups and individuals construct *different* perspectives, then we may be led to conclude that the accounts produced by ethnographers are simply one version of the world that is no more valid than others.[18] This tendency towards rejection of the possibility of representation (which I shall call anti-realism) has been reinforced by the influence of a wide range of philosophical ideas, including phenomenology, hermeneutics, structuralism, post-structuralism, and Wittgensteinian language philosophy.[19]

One of the most recent products of this anti-realism has been scrutiny of ethnographic and other accounts as texts, looking at the rhetorical devices that are used to 'create' the world portrayed. The suggestion is that conventional ethnographic work is wedded to a spurious realism. It claims to represent the setting studied 'as it is'. But this is not possible because we have no access to an independent reality; all we have are interpretations, and the ethnographer's account is just as much an interpretation as are those of the people that he or she is studying. The critics claim that, in order to establish that their accounts represent reality, ethnographers rely on rhetorical devices that are analogous to those employed by travel writers and realist novelists such as Dickens or Zola. For example, anthropologists sometimes include in their accounts a description of their first sight of the setting they were to study, thereby 'proving' in a narrative way that they have 'really' been there. Similarly, one finds superfluous details in ethnographic accounts, information that is not necessary to support the analysis. This is included, it is suggested, to give an added sense of realism to the account, just as novelists like Dickens spend much time describing the details of the settings in which events take place as well as of the appearance and manner of the people involved.[20]

These critics do not reject the use of rhetorical devices. Indeed, they argue that rhetoric cannot be avoided. What they want is more honest rhetoric, rhetoric that does not pretend to an unattainable realism. Such arguments have motivated some novel kinds of ethnographic writing; for example, texts that incorporate the voices of the people studied in a more substantial and less controlled way than is common in conventional ethnographic accounts.[21]

From a variety of points of view, then, conventional ethnographic research has come under criticism in recent times not for failing to be scientific but for seeking to adopt the scientific model. Its commitment to describing and explaining the social world, rather than seeking to change it, has been rejected by some. The relationship between ethnography and the people studied has been attacked as exploitative. And ethnography's very capacity to represent social reality 'in its own terms' has been challenged. Response to such criticisms has been mixed. In general, the reaction has been to accept the criticisms to various degrees; though there is little sign as yet of any major transformation in ethnographic practice.

CONCLUSION

In this chapter I have outlined the character of ethnography as a set of research strategies as well as the more philosophical ideas that support those strategies. In addition, I have looked at methodological debates about ethnography, both those concerned with criticism that it is not scientific enough and those centred on arguments that the model of natural science is inappropriate for ethnography.

If what I have said makes it sound as if ethnography is currently in crisis, that is not far from the truth. Most obvious is the crisis of fragmentation: there is no single ethnographic paradigm or community, but a diversity of approaches claiming to be ethnographic (and often disagreeing with one another). More fundamentally, though, the crisis stems from deep, unresolved questions about the nature of our knowledge of the social world and about the purposes which that knowledge can and should serve. These questions face all social and educational researchers, not just ethnographers. Ethnographers are beginning to wrestle with them, but there is little consensus about solutions.

What is presented in the remainder of this book represents one attempt to deal with these problems in the context of providing a guide to reading ethnographic research. It is necessarily somewhat tentative, and controversial. In the next chapter I begin by looking at how we should set about understanding the claims made in ethnographic texts.

NOTES

1. I shall use some of these terms as synonyms for 'ethnography' in this book.

2. For a brief overview of the history of ethnography in the context of social and cultural anthropology, see Wax (1971). Darnell (1977) provides a more detailed history, and Darnell (1974) collects together extracts from early anthropological work and from historical accounts of its development. For a history of twentieth-century Anglo-American sociology that focuses on methodological approaches, see Madge (1963). Burgess (1982, ch. 1) provides a useful brief account of the recent history of ethnography in both anthropology and sociology.

3. Malinowski was not the only figure in this movement, nor did his research practice conform very closely to the ethnographic ideal that he recommended. See Kaberry (1957) and Wax (1972).

4. For detailed discussions of the Chicago School, see Bulmer (1984), Harvey (1987), and Hammersley (1989a).

5. For accounts of the US and British traditions of community study, see Bell and Newby (1971). Frankenberg (1966) provides a systematic presentation of some of the British findings. See also Cole (1977) on the anthropology of European society. On the Lynds, see Madge (1963, ch. 5).

6. For examples of this research, see Whyte (1981), Rose (1962), Becker *et al.* (1961 and 1969). For attempts to codify and develop ethnographic method in this period, see Glaser and Strauss (1967), McCall and Simmons (1969), and Becker (1970).

7. For brief histories of qualitative research in Britain, see Payne *et al.* (1981) and Strong (1988). Atkinson *et al.* (1988) provide a review of British qualitative research on education.

8. The use of the term 'naturalism' is ambiguous in the methodological literature. It is sometimes used to refer to the adoption of the natural science model, sometimes (as here) to indicate a concern with capturing the nature of the phenomena studied (which may well imply using different methods to those characteristic of the natural sciences). See Matza (1969) for a discussion of the term and references to its diversity of usage. For a clear account of the covering law model, see Lessnoff (1974) or Keat and Urry (1975). On the pattern model of explanation, see the discussion and references in Hammersley (1989a).

9. It should be said, though, that ethnographers do not believe that understanding requires that they become full members of the group(s) being studied. Indeed, most believe that this must not occur if a valid and useful account is to be produced. The ethnographer must try to be both outsider and insider, staying on the margins of the group both socially and intellectually. This is because what is required is *both* an outside *and* an inside view. For this reason it is sometimes emphasised that, besides seeking to 'understand', the ethnographer must also try to see familiar settings as 'anthropologically strange', as they would be seen by

someone from another society, adopting what we might call the Martian perspective.

10. I cannot cover the full range of criticism and response, the aim is simply to give a flavour of the sort of argument and counter-argument that has taken place. I am also not intending to endorse the credibility of either criticisms or defences. The issues involved are often more complex and difficult than such exchanges suggest. I shall discuss some of these issues in more detail later.

11. Kuhn did not deny the role of rational judgement entirely, simply that it provided the sole and certain basis for paradigm shift. (See, especially, the postscript to the second edition of his book: Kuhn, 1970.)

12. For reviews of these arguments, and references, see Siegel (1987), Tiles (1988), and Newton-Smith (1990).

13. On these arguments, see Passmore (1978).

14. See, for example, Habermas (1973). For an overview of Habermas's work, see McCarthy (1978).

15. For references and one assessment of feminist methodology, see Hammersley (1990e).

16. However, see Smart's comments about this in relation to her research on solicitors (Smart, 1984).

17. For references and an assessment of the argument for practitioner research in the area of education, see Hammersley and Scarth (1990).

18. One influential version of this argument is to be found in the writings of some ethnomethodologists.

19. While these ideas differ in many ways and are by no means all straightforwardly anti-realist, collectively their influence has encouraged anti-realism in sociology. For a useful introductory discussion of these intellectual movements, see Anderson *et al.* (1986).

20. See for example Clifford (1988), Clifford and Marcus (1986) and Marcus and Fischer (1986).

21. See, for example, Krieger (1983), Shostak (1981), Crapanzano (1980).

CHAPTER 2

Understanding ethnographic accounts

We may read ethnographic studies for a variety of reasons, but for most purposes a first requirement is that we understand what the author is claiming and on what grounds. These may seem relatively straightforward matters, fixed in black and white on the page before us. But what is on the page is simply print. To get at what we are interested in we have to *interpret* what is written. As we shall see, this is not always a simple matter; and some of the reasons for this lie in the very nature of ethnographic texts themselves.

MODES OF ETHNOGRAPHIC WRITING

There has never been a standard format of presentation for ethnographic research reports. They rarely follow the structure that is recommended for quantitative reports: presentation of the research problem and hypotheses; account of the methods employed; statement of the findings; discussion of the implications. In recent years the nature of ethnographic texts has been given increasing attention.[1] As a result, some ethnographers have become more self-conscious about the way they write, and the assumptions about knowledge and the world that are involved.

One of the fruits of this new self-consciousness has been the identification of several common *modes* of ethnographic writing, all of which may occur within the same text. One of the most common is what is referred to as ethnographic 'realism' or 'naturalism'.[2] Here, the account is written in such a way as to give the reader the impression that he or she is observing the scene described. The researcher is often absent from these portrayals, as if merely a camera. Here is van Maanen's summary description of this form of writing:

Basically, the narrator of realist tales poses as an impersonal conduit who, unlike missionaries, administrators, journalists, or unabashed members of the culture themselves, passes on more-or-less objective data in a measured intellectual style that is uncontaminated by personal bias, political goals, or moral judgments. (van Maanen, 1988: 47)

He notes that such writing includes 'precise, mundane details', takes account of the 'native point of view' by including quotations from informants, but maintains the researcher's 'interpretive omnipotence' in that he or she 'has the last word'.

This sort of ethnographic writing is often very close in character to that which is typical of histories, biographies, and even novels. Here is a very clear example of naturalistic writing of this kind:

At the end of Winston Street is a yellow wall with a number of graffiti – a list of boys, *Jimmy, Norman, Eddie, Marvin, Robert*, and a list of girls next to it, *Barbie, Debbie, Sarah, Peaches, Janice.* There is a secretive *Leroy loves somebody*, and a couple of four-letter words scrawled by an uncertain hand. A little to the side, the message is that *Your mother drink wild irish rose*, with the reply *So do your cat.* Wild Irish rose is the drink of the winos, 'wineheads' or 'juiceheads' in ghetto parlance.

Winston Street, Washington D.C., is a narrow, one-way ghetto street, one block long and lined by brick row houses, two or three stories high and in varying states of repair. In the windows of some of them are flower pots, bright curtains or even venetian blinds. Others have broken blinds, dirty plastic sheets, or nothing at all. Sometimes a house is condemned as unfit to live in, and its doors and windows are covered with boards. It is largely a residential street, and since it is not really a thoroughfare, its pedestrian and auto traffic is largely confined to the street's own residents and their visitors. At the corners of Winston Street and the surrounding streets are small business establishments: groceries, liquor stores, carry-out food shops, variety stores, laundromats, shoeshine shops, barber shops, beauty salons; all very modest in appearance. These are the establishments which cater to the day-to-day needs, and supply the few luxuries, of ghetto living. The consumption of liquor is considerable. The carry-outs find most of their customers among the many single men who cannot prepare food in their rented rooms, as well as among the children and adolescents who spend much of whatever money they can get on extra food and goodies. Variety stores sell candy, school equipment, cheap toys, and a variety of other inexpensive odds and ends. The carry-outs, the barber shops, and the shoeshine shops serve not only their manifest function but are also the hangouts, the centers of sociability, of teenagers and adult men. To serve as locales of leisure, they add some more items to their furnishings: newspapers, vending machines for cigarettes and soft drinks, a pinball machine, a juke box, a public telephone. No one establishment would have them all, some would have none of this, but many have some of it (. . .). (Hannerz, 1969: 19)

These are the opening paragraphs of Ulf Hannerz's book *Soulside*, a study of black ghetto life in Washington DC in the late 1960s. Extracts like this abound in ethnographic accounts, especially where the setting investigated is being introduced. However, most naturalistic writing is not as concretely descriptive as this. The central goal of ethnographic research is often conceptualised as providing an *analytic, thick* or *theoretical* description, rather than just the relatively concrete, commonsensical kind illustrated above. Such descriptions (whether of whole societies, small communities, organisations, spatial locations or 'social worlds') must not only remain close to the concrete reality of particular events, but also reveal general features of the life of a particular category of people, group or setting, or even of human social life as a whole. As the terminology implies, 'theoretical descriptions' claim to be simultaneously descriptions and theories, and their theoretical elements cannot be extracted from them without coming to seem 'commonplace and vacant' (Geertz, 1973: 25). Theoretical descriptions are, then, laced with reflections about the significance of what is described.

Later on in his book, Hannerz presents some examples of conversations between men hanging out on street corners. In seeking to understand them he draws on a variety of theoretical and empirical literature in order to highlight similarities and differences between these conversations and those characteristic of, for example, middle class parties. Here is a brief extract from his discussion which illustrates the nature of such 'theoretical description':

The men seem preoccupied with creating and maintaining a definition of natural masculinity which they can all share. By seizing on individual experiences of kinds which they have all had, they 'talk through' and thereby construct the social reality of the typical Ghetto Man, a fact of life larger than any one of them. This Ghetto Man is a bit of a hero, a bit of a villain, and a bit of a fool, yet none of them all the way. He is in fact a kind of a trickster – uncertainty personified, a creature fluctuating between competence and incompetence, success and failure, good and evil. He applies his mother wit or is plainly lucky sometimes (. . .) and this helps him come out victorious or at least unscathed. But not all the time, for native wit and luck have their limits (. . .) Anyway, when Ghetto Man succeeds, he is a hero, considering his limited skills and powers in an environment full of adversaries; if he fails it is natural because he was up to no good. (Hannerz, 1969: 112)

What Hannerz presents here is an interpretation of the stories exchanged by the street corner men he observed, drawing out what he takes their significance to be for the nature of men's lives in the ghetto. Often theoretical descriptions involve the categorisation of the phenomena described under some general concept, perhaps one that is novel to the account. Thus, Hannerz refers to the story-telling he describes as 'mythmaking', something that we can expect to find in other settings, not just in ghettoes but elsewhere too. In these ways, theoretical hypotheses, interpretations and conclusions are woven into the account as part of the description.

Ethnographic accounts rarely, if ever, consist solely of naturalistic writing of these kinds. At some point, often near the beginning, there will usually be discussion of the focus of the research, why it is of significance, what methods were employed etc. And at the end there may be a summary of the findings and some conclusions. Much of this surrounding material may be interpreted as designed to assure the reader of the importance and objectivity of the account, and for this reason I shall refer to it as writing in the 'legitimatory' mode. It will usually contain useful information about how and why the research was done.

In recent years an additional form of writing, besides the naturalistic and legitimatory, has become common among ethnographers: what has been called the 'confessional' mode, in which the 'inside story' of the research is told. The anthropologist Clifford Geertz refers to this as 'the diary disease', so popular has it become (Geertz, 1988: 90). In its fully developed form the confessional mode may include reports of incidents that are potentially discrediting for the researcher. For example, in one of the earliest examples of this genre William Foote Whyte reports his naivety at the start of his research on an Italian area in Boston, USA, in the late 1930s, and his later participation in election-rigging (Whyte, 1981). In a more recent example, John Johnson presents an extended argument for the importance of researchers showing the personal side of research, and provides an inside account of his own research on social workers, including his physical reactions to the stress of fieldwork (Johnson, 1975). Of course, while such accounts purport to give the inside story of the research, they are selective. What is included depends on what the writer judges to be relevant (and on what he or she is prepared to admit!). Also, they are accounts from one particular point of view, that of the researcher. Nevertheless, such research biographies offer information about the researcher and the course of the research that may not be available elsewhere, and which may be very important for any assessment of the findings of the research.

The naturalistic, legitimatory and confessional are the most common modes of writing to be found in ethnographic accounts. The first two are present in most ethnographies, with the naturalistic mode predominating. More confessional writing may also be present, though research biographies are often published separately from the study to which they relate. There are sometimes deviations from this pattern, however. For instance, Wieder provides a conventional ethnographic account of the code of belief and behaviour that he found in a halfway house for ex-prisoners in Los Angeles; but then in the second part of his book, under the influence of ethnomethodology, sets out to show that this 'convict code' was not something separate from the behaviour that he observed and which explains it (as his initial account suggested), but rather was created and recreated in and through the everyday actions that he observed, and through his own interpretations (Wieder, 1974). Other ethnographic writings depart from naturalism by abandoning the voice of a narrator. Krieger's study of a women's community is an example of this. Her whole account consists of the words of the women themselves, derived from interviews and reported in indirect speech. Other novel approaches have involved developments of the life history approach. Crapanzano, for example, presents the life history of Tuhami, an illiterate Moroccan tile maker, in such a way as to try to avoid what he sees as the tendency of conventional ethnography to 'render bizarre, exotic, or downright irrational what would have been ordinary in its own context' (p. 8). This requires paying attention both to the rhetorical devices by which Tuhami tells his stories and to those that Crapanzano himself employs to locate them; as well as to the active role that the latter played in eliciting the life history. Crapanzano asks his readers 'to abandon for the moment (their) assumptions about reality' so that they will share 'some of the anguished puzzlement I felt, and presumably Tuhami felt, as we tried to make sense of each other' (Crapanzano 1980: 23).[3]

I shall not give these deviant modes of presentation much attention, since they are still relatively rare. However, it is important to recognise the criticisms of more conventional modes that have motivated them. The mix of naturalistic and legitimatory writing that makes up most ethnographic accounts is closely wedded to the three assumptions that I identified as basic to ethnography in Chapter 1; and it is some aspects of those assumptions, and especially of naturalism and discovery, that advocates of these new modes of writing challenge. Central here, as I noted in Chapter 1, is rejection of ethnographers' claims to describe an independent reality. In laying the basis for his analysis of the textual strategies used by ethnographers, van Maanen illustrates this anti-realism. He comments that:

culture is not strictly speaking a scientific object, but is created, as is the reader's view of it, by the active construction of a text. (van Maanen, 1988: 7)

While I do not accept this anti-realism, there is no doubt that it points to an important problem facing conventional ethnography.[4] The naturalistic mode of writing portrays communities, settings and people without explicit indication of how the description was produced, for what purpose, and what alternative descriptions have been or could reasonably have been considered. The implication seems to be that what is provided is a more or less accurate *reproduction* of the phenomena described. There are several reasons to question this.

First, it is never possible to reproduce a phenomenon by describing it. Descriptions are always selective, they focus on some aspects of objects and omit others. As a result, there are always multiple, non-contradictory, true accounts possible of any phenomenon. Given the selective character of ethnographic description, we need to know the basis for selection. Ethnographic descriptions in the naturalistic mode typically do not make this explicit.

Second, naturalism effectively assumes that validity of descriptions can be ensured by close contact with the phenomenon being described. Much legitimatory writing in ethnographic studies is concerned with establishing that the ethnographer has been to the place and seen what is described. Geertz remarks about anthropological ethnography:

> . . . the ability of anthropologists to get us to take what they say seriously (has to do) (. . .) with their capacity to convince us that what they say is a result of their having actually penetrated (or, if you prefer, having been penetrated by) another form of life, of having (. . .) truly 'been there'. (Geertz, 1988: 4–5)

Van Maanen refers to this as the 'doctrine of immaculate perception' (van Maanen, 1988: 74); and, as the pun implies, this form of legitimation is illusory. What is provided, in effect, is an account of what it is believed the researcher *would* have 'seen' in the field had he or she looked at it with the concerns which structured the subsequent analysis. It is not uncommon for the focus of the final report of a piece of ethnographic research to be quite different from that of the researcher when he or she was in the field. On top of this, much that is described by ethnographers cannot be *seen* in any straightforward way: it is a product of cognitive interpretation. What ethnographers 'discover' in the course of fieldwork is a product of complex processes of interpretation, as well as of social interaction between themselves and the various people participating in the setting observed, including those acting as their informants. It is never a simple reflection of what exists.

From these points of view, ethnographic naturalism can be systematically misleading. This highlights the need for careful reading of ethnographic texts. If we read such accounts in a relatively passive way, we may be lulled into accepting what they portray at face value. More careful, and perhaps repeated, reading is necessary if we are to understand them effectively.

A STRATEGY FOR READING

To start with we must be clear about what it is that we are trying to understand. I shall assume that what we are interested in is a particular account, not the research process that produced it.[5] A single research project may produce more than one research report – for example, articles focusing on various aspects of the phenomenon investigated, perhaps a book, perhaps also a research biography. Furthermore, as I noted, because of the exploratory and developmental character of ethnography, there may be a difference between the original focus of the research and the focus of the research report(s) it produces. Equally, there may be a discrepancy between the terms in which the research focus is justified and the motives that originally inspired the research. For example, Punch justifies his focus on policing in a central area of Amsterdam on the general grounds that the problems of policing in metropolitan city centres have been largely ignored by Anglo-American work on the police, and that there is virtually no Dutch research on policing at all. However, his more confessional discussion of how his research came to be located in Amsterdam reveals the element of contingency frequently to be found in the selection of ethnographic research topics and sites. He reports his failure to get permission to study the police in Britain, that he had spent some time in the Netherlands on a research fellowship, and that his wife is Dutch. And he comments that his interest in Amsterdam's city centre stemmed from his knowledge that police stations there would be busy:

Given my limited time, I wanted to observe as much as possible and had little inclination to spend my time in a sleepy suburb with traffic accidents and violations as the major diversions from tedium and drinking coffee. (Punch, 1979: 3)

Such information about the research process is relevant to assessing the research reports it produces. And it will usually be worthwhile to look at other accounts deriving from the same research (and especially any research biography) if these are available and accessible. However, these are useful only insofar as they illuminate the account we are trying to understand.

In setting out to understand an ethnographic account it is important that we distinguish between various aspects of it that serve different functions. These aspects deal with: the research focus; the case(s) studied; the methods of data collection and analysis used; the major claims and the evidence provided for them; and, finally, the conclusions drawn about the research focus. These elements may not be clearly indicated or differentiated by the writer, but it is useful to distinguish between them, as I shall try to show.

In the remainder of this chapter I shall look at each of these five aspects of ethnographic research reports.

1. *THE RESEARCH FOCUS*

I shall use the term 'research focus' to refer to the most general set of phenomena about which the study makes claims, and the aspects of them that are of concern. For instance, the focus of Hannerz's *Soulside* is various features of the culture of black ghettos in the United States, plus some of their causes and consequences.

More specifically, we can think of the focus as the general set of questions that the study addresses. And, it is important to distinguish between the different sorts of question that might be addressed. These may be descriptive, explanatory, predictive, evaluative or prescriptive. They may also include empirical generalisations and/or theoretical claims.[6] The distinctions among these types of question are rarely made by ethnographers and thus are not usually clearly marked in ethnographic texts. Indeed, as I noted earlier, ethnographic work is often guided by the notion of theoretical description, which seeks to combine description, explanation and theory; and sometimes incorporates evaluative and prescriptive elements too. However, in my view it is important to recognise the diversity of focus and product to be found among ethnographic accounts, not least because the different types of claim place varying requirements on the researcher, in terms of the sort of evidence that is required to support them; and they therefore have implications for what evidence the reader should expect. Of course, a study may aim at more than one type of product, in which case we must interpret it in terms of the requirements implied by all of its goals.

Besides the focus itself, we must also look out for any rationale that the author offers as to why the focus of the study is important, and thus why the conclusions might be of interest to us. Thus, in the introduction to *Soulside* Ulf Hannerz notes that a considerable amount of social science research has been done on black ghettos, but claims that its character has led it to be largely ignored. He reports the complaints of some black critics that such research has failed to capture the nature of ghetto life. Indeed, he notes how those wishing to understand the experience of black people living in the US often turn to novels and poetry rather than to the work of social scientists. He comments that:

perhaps anthropology (by which in this context he can be taken to mean ethnography) can give a more insightful picture of (the) human side to the ghetto condition than other social sciences do. The willfulness, endurance, strength and humanity (. . .) can be understood only within the grassroots context, and anthropology as a form of consciousness may be better able to inquire into these personal terms of life while at the same time remaining more systematic than the literary view of the black experience. (Hannerz, 1969: 14).[7]

Most ethnographic accounts provide some explicit statement of their focus and of the assumed significance of the study. Usually this occurs at the beginning of the account; though it need not occur right at the start, and relevant material may be found in any part of the account and in other sources too.

In book-length studies the rationale for the research focus may amount to one or more chapters, including reviews of the literature which identify the gap that the study is intended to fill. As another illustration of the sorts of information that may be provided about focus and rationale, here is an example taken from Strong's book *The Ceremonial Order of the Clinic*:

This is a book about the meetings that doctors have with parents when a child is sick or needs medical inspection. (. . .) It says nothing about the medicine involved in all this and very little about people's feelings, opinions or perceptions. These things are interesting but they are not my interest here. My concern is with ceremonies: with the social form of the occasion and the sorts of identity tacitly claimed by each party and conferred upon the other.

(. . .) The point of my description is this: here are over a thousand separate occasions on which parents met doctors and met them in all kinds of different circumstances, and yet the manner of their meeting, the ceremonial order of the occasion, was pretty much the same no matter what other things might vary. One can go further. The outward form of their relationship took just the one shape, give or take a few minor alterations, in all of the Scottish consultations and in most of the American ones too.

So here we have something fairly powerful, a manner of meeting, a mode of being doctor and parent, which was used across a great range of contingencies and particularities; this mode – the 'bureaucratic format' – is my main topic and I shall try to describe its nature, its origins, the methods by which it was sustained and the actual fit between this outward show and the matters which it clothed.

In doing all this I have several aims, some modest, others less so. One is to comment on medical work with children and their parents, another is to reflect more generally on medical consultations, for although paediatrics is one small segment of the clinical world its methods and dilemmas may well have their counterparts in other areas of medicine. There may also be something for sociologists. Medical consultations are merely one in a myriad of those occasions and events which sociologists study, and the frames or formats used therein may be of little interest save to specialists in the field of service relationships. Nevertheless, since the master of ceremony, Erving Goffman himself, has paid little attention to the study of any one order, the careful delineation of a form may still have something to say about formats in general and the structures which shape our daily lives.

Statements like this are not always immediately accessible. They assume background knowledge (in this case, for instance, about who Erving Goffman is and what 'ceremonial order' might mean). Like all writing they are directed at a particular audience about whom assumptions regarding knowledge and interest are made, and it may be that as readers we do not match those assumptions. However, even though there may be parts of what the author says that are obscure to us we shall usually be able to get the gist of what is being focused on, and the sorts of questions that are being asked, and why.

Strong gives some indication of the focus of his study in the very first sentence quoted: '(. . .) meetings that doctors have with parents when a child is sick or needs medical inspection.' The remainder of that first paragraph spells out the aspect of that phenomenon in which he is interested: his account is designed to answer the questions, 'what is the social form of the occasion?', and 'what sorts of identity are claimed by each party and are conferred on the other?'. And we can note that these seem to be descriptive questions.

The next two paragraphs of the extract are confusing from our point of view, since they summarise one of the findings of the study (that the 'bureaucratic format' was the dominant one). Such mixing of focus and findings is not uncommon in ethnographic studies, and sometimes it is not easy to tell what belongs where. But, as far as is possible, it is worth keeping these apart.

The final paragraph of the extract from Strong's book hints at the rationale for the focus of his study, but in doing so it complicates the identification of focus that we made on the basis of the first paragraph. The object that we identified earlier (medical work with children and their parents) is now itself subsumed under the headings of three broader foci: medical consultations of all kinds, service relationships, and (implicitly) human relationships in general. Ethnographic studies can have more than one focus, then, and identifying them may require careful reading. In subsequent analyses attention will need to be given to how well the study addresses each of its foci. We should note that the rationales for these different foci may also differ. Thus, in the conclusion to his book Strong presents both practical recommendations about how paediatric consultations might be improved as well as conclusions relating to the theoretical literature dealing with interactional formats of all kinds. His study, therefore, has both practical and theoretical rationales.

What I have quoted from Strong's study is only a small part of a lengthy process of scene-setting, which takes up not only the Preface (from which the extract comes) but also the first chapter, in which he discusses other literature dealing with contacts between staff and patients, pointing out that it neglects the features he is concerned with and outlining what he takes to be the consequences of this.

The first task, then, in seeking to understand an ethnographic text is to identify the focus of the research and the rationale for it. The next is to identify the case(s) investigated.

2. *THE CASE(S) INVESTIGATED*

We need to be careful in distinguishing the focus of the research from the cases studied. I defined the focus above as the most general set of phenomena about which the study makes claims. Usually, this will be a *type* of phenomena or some large *aggregate* of cases. For example, black ghettos in US cities, paediatric consultations, service encounters, etc. By 'the cases studied', on the other hand, I mean the phenomena specifically located in place and time about which data were collected. For example, while Hannerz drew conclusions about black ghetto life in general, his data relate to the people of Winston Street, Washington DC, during some period in the 1960s. So, black ghetto culture was his focus, and the Winston Street community at that time was his case.

I noted in Chapter 1 that ethnographic research typically studies a small number of cases, often only one. In this respect Hannerz's study is typical. Strong's study of medical encounters, on the other hand, is unusual from this point of view since his analysis is based on data from 1,120 encounters between doctors and parents. Obviously, the smaller the size of the case the more examples can be studied with the same resources (other things being equal), but such a large number of cases is rare in ethnographic research.

It is worth noting that ethnographic accounts often intermingle discussion of focus and case. An example is Atkinson's discussion of the clinical years of the medical education of doctors, where the writing moves at will between the focus (the experiences and perspectives of medical students in general) and the sample of Edinburgh medical students that Atkinson studied in the early 1970s. Even so, it is usually relatively straightforward to distinguish between focus and case, not least because the former is generally of significance for a wide audience, whereas the latter is not. I doubt whether many of us are interested, for its own sake, in information about the lives of the Winston Street inhabitants of the 1960s or about some Edinburgh medical students in the 1970s. Whatever interest we have stems from what we may infer from this information, for example, about ghetto life and medical students in more general terms. There are exceptions to this, however. Nigel Fielding's study of the National Front is a case in point. He presents his study as an investigation of political deviance and discusses the criteria for selecting a group for investigation of this topic. However, clearly, a study of the National Front (even though limited in time-span, and now out of date) is of general interest in itself, as Fielding recognises:

This party meets my criteria for a political group whose study can contribute to an understanding of (. . .) political deviance while also being worthy of description and analysis in its own right. (Fielding, 1981: 7)

For the most part, though, the cases studied by ethnographers are of rather limited interest in themselves (even though they are or were of great interest to the people involved). And usually, of course, their identity is disguised from readers through the use of pseudonyms, so that we *cannot* easily identify the actual case studied.

Sometimes the focus of the research may apparently be restricted to the case studied even though that case is not of obvious general interest. For example, some of my own work explicitly limits its claims to what occurred in a particular inner-city secondary modern school in the early 1970s (Hammersley, 1974). Such a cautious limitation of focus is disingenuous, it now seems to me. After all, why would my study warrant publication if it did not have implications for some more widely relevant focus? In such cases I think we must conclude that the focus is different to the case studied, but is left implicit. Where this occurs, we must try to identify what seems likely to have been the intended focus.

Most accounts provide at least some information about the case(s) selected and the reasons for its/their selection; and further information may be obtained from other sources, notably research biographies. Of course, the information that could be provided is virtually endless. What it is necessary to know depends, in part, on our familiarity with similar cases. Thus, a study of primary school classrooms does not need to give most readers much information about the setting. Here is what French and French provide in their study of gender imbalances in such classrooms:

The data to be considered comprise a verbatim transcription of a fourth-year junior school lesson (pupils aged 10 and 11 years). The lesson is one from an extended series that one of us (JF) observed and recorded as part of an ethnographic study of gender differentiation in primary classrooms. (. . .) The lesson is organized as a teacher–class discussion of the topic 'What I do on Mondays and what I would like to do on Mondays'. In an earlier lesson pupils had addressed this topic in writing, but their essay answers proved unsatisfactory to the teacher. The present lesson therefore covers a number of points which, the teacher explains, he would like to have seen included. After the lesson, pupils make a second attempt at the essay. The class contained 29 pupils, 16 girls and 13 boys. The teacher was male. (French and French, 1984: 128)

By contrast, an article on dock pilferage by longshoremen in St Johns, Newfoundland, provides over five pages of description of the port and the different types of work in which longshoremen (or dock workers) are involved (Mars, 1974); and it is clear that such information is required if most British (and probably even most Canadian) readers are to be able to understand the findings.

In addition to information about the case studied, we must also look out for any indication of why it is believed to be of relevance to the research focus, or at least the basis on which it was selected. This may involve the claim that the case is typical of some type or population of cases. For example, Westley justifies the case he studied in his investigation of police violence as follows:

The police department was located in a small mid-western industrial city. At the time of the study this city seemed similar to large urban centers in having a slum area, a sizable Negro sub-community, major traffic problems, a system of political patronage, and a high crime rate. This city was not, of course, representative of major urban centers in the United States for its size, economic composition, and political influence sharply differentiated it from them. But as far as the police are concerned, it posed most of the major problems encountered by police departments in the larger cities in traffic, in political corruption, in crime, in ethnic relations, and so forth. Its policemen reacted as if they were urban policemen. (Westley, 1970: xi–xii)

Westley seems to be arguing here that the city he studied was typical of others in most respects that are important for generalisation of his findings; even though it is clearly atypical in other respects.

Alternatively, cases are sometimes justified precisely on the basis of their atypicality. Cicourel and Kitsuse studied Lakeside High, a school that they point out was not representative of US high schools, not just in serving an exclusively high income neighbourhood but also in its large size, bureaucratic structure and professionalised counselling service. However, they argue that this school was in the vanguard of changes that were taking place among US high schools so that more and more schools would become similar to Lakeside High in respects relevant to their research findings. On this basis, they claim that their findings will be generalisable to many other schools in the future.

As we shall see, the question of the relationship between case and focus is complex. I shall discuss this further when looking at conclusions below.

3. METHODS USED

Having identified the research focus, the case(s) studied and the rationales for them, the next task is to look at the means by which the investigation was carried out: what sources of data were employed?; what were the relationships between the researcher and the people studied?; what analytic techniques were used?; etc.

As I noted in Chapter 1, it is characteristic of ethnography to employ a *range* of data sources: reports of observation and perhaps also of participation; audio- and video-recordings and transcripts; interviews; documents; and perhaps also questionnaire responses and/or test results may be involved. But even this range of types of data does not capture the full potential variation.

Observation, for example, can take a variety of forms: it may be covert or overt, to varying degrees and varying in relation to different groups of participants; and it may involve participation in an established role in the setting (marginal or more central) or in a 'visitor' or specially created researcher role. At one extreme, for example, there is the covert research of Melville Dalton on *Men who Manage*, where only a few of the people in the settings knew that he was carrying out research, and even they knew little about it (Dalton, 1959). At the other end of the spectrum is the already mentioned work of the Swede Ulf Hannerz in a black ghetto community, a man whose very appearance and accent would presumably have marked him out for everyone as a visitor.

Similarly, interviewing can vary in the degree to which the interviewer structures the interaction, how directive the questions are, etc. Sometimes ethnographers use relatively structured interviews close in form to those characteristic of survey research, in order to gain the same information from a large number of participants. More commonly, though, ethnographic interviews are open-ended, designed to explore the perspectives of the people concerned. Even within such exploratory interviews, however, there may be some directive questions designed to test responses or even to provoke.[8]

Documents may also vary in character. They may be elicited by the researcher or may have been produced for other purposes; and extant documents include personal diaries and letters as well as public documents like official reports.

Such variations in the character of the data employed must be noted since they can have important implications for the kinds of threats to validity likely to operate on the findings. For this reason it is important to summarise any information provided by the researcher about the methods and data he or she used, following up references to other materials relating to the research where more detail may be given. Here, as elsewhere, there may be a gap between the information we feel we need and that provided.

4. IDENTIFYING THE MAIN ARGUMENTS AND EVIDENCE

The most central task in understanding an ethnographic study is to identify its main findings and the evidence presented in support of them.[9] I shall deal with these separately.

Main claims

Above, I drew a distinction between research focus and case (or cases) studied. Corresponding to this, I shall also make a distinction between the conclusions of a study (which relate to its focus) and the major claims (which relate to the case). So, in looking for the major claims of a study we are looking for those findings that refer specifically to the case studied, leaving any that refer beyond the case for later consideration as conclusions. Of course, there will often be considerable overlap in content between the major claims and the conclusions; that which is found in the case studied perhaps being generalised to other cases. But the distinction is important because assessing the validity of such generalisations is an added task over and above the assessment of the claims themselves.

Within any research report there will be a host of claims made, and the task of identifying the main ones involves detecting the structure of the account so as to see which are superordinate and which subordinate. Usually this is not too difficult: authors will indicate to one degree or another which are the most important points they are making and how the others relate to them. We can also rely on our understanding of the focus and goal of the account, though it is always possible that we may find it necessary to revise this or to conclude that there are inconsistencies in the report.

In seeking to identify the main arguments in an ethnographic study, a useful starting point is of course any summary provided by the writer. Summaries may occur in conclusions at the end of articles (or in concluding chapters of books) or they may come earlier. Here, for example, is the author's summary (provided quite near the beginning of the article) of an account of the effects of variations in teachers' expectations on pupil performance in the kindergarten and early grades of an inner-city school in a black US community:

The argument may be succinctly stated in five propositions.

First, the kindergarten teacher possessed a roughly constructed 'ideal type' as to what characteristics were necessary for any given student to achieve 'success' both in the public school and in the larger society. These characteristics appeared to be, in significant part, related to social class criteria.

Second, upon first meeting her students at the beginning of the school year, subjective evaluations were made of the students as to possession or absence of the desired traits necessary for anticipated 'success'. On the basis of the evaluation, the class was divided into groups expected to succeed (termed by the teacher 'fast learners') and those anticipated to fail (termed 'slow learners').

Third, differential treatment was accorded to the two groups in the classroom, with the group designated as 'fast learners' receiving the majority of the teaching time, reward-directed behavior, and attention from the teacher. Those designated as 'slow learners' were taught infrequently, subjected to more frequent control-oriented behavior, and received little if any supportive behavior from the teacher.

Fourth, the interactional patterns between the teacher and the various groups in her class became rigidified, taking on caste-like characteristics, during the course of the school year, with the gap in completion of academic material between the two groups widening as the school year progressed.

Fifth, a similar process occurred in later years of schooling, but the teachers no longer relied on subjectively interpreted data as the basis for ascertaining differences in students. Rather, they were able to utilize a variety of informational sources related to past performance as the basis for classroom grouping. (Rist, 1970: 413–14; I have introduced paragraphs into this extract for purposes of clarification.)

Such summaries are extremely useful in giving us a sense of what the overall argument of a study is. However, we should not rely on them entirely. Sometimes, we shall find that, in our judgement at least, they are not entirely accurate or complete. For example, in my view Rist's summary of his main claims omits a significant one: that the pupils themselves responded differentially to the teacher's behaviour towards them, in ways that reinforced the teacher's expectations. Also, where Rist refers to two groups of children in the summary (fast and slow learners) in fact the teachers he studied each divided their classes into three groups, though still ranging from 'fast' to 'slow'.

While summaries provided by the author are useful, then, they are no substitute for one's own careful reading of the whole text. At the very least, one may find differences of emphasis between the summary and the actual account, and sometimes there can be important discrepancies. And it is worth noting that the authors may also mix what I have distinguished as claims and conclusions.

To illustrate the sort of argumentative structure one is likely to find in ethnographic studies here is an extended extract from a book reporting an ethnographic study of juvenile courts. This extract deals primarily with one of the two courts studied (Countyside, rather than City, Court). As an exercise you might find it useful to note what you take to be the main points as you read the extract.[10]

ABUSING JUSTICE: THE IMPACT OF SOCIAL CLASS
It would be a naive argument that the social class differential between magistrates and defendants was in itself the key issue in the 'objectification' of the defendants and the creation of punitive justice. To say that magistrates are middle aged and middle class seems almost a truism since it is clearly observable and documented (Burney, 1979). Most criminal defendants are from working-class backgrounds. In Countyside the gulf, the social distance between the bench and defendants, was considerable and clearly brought home by the frequency with which magistrates had to quit the bench abruptly for specific hearings because they knew defendants and their parents personally from acting as employer, head teacher, councillor and so on. The magistrates were, in the main, professional or propertied people and the defendants were, by and large, from one of the most deprived urban areas in the United Kingdom. It is obviously dangerous to generalize but so often did defendants and parents have the appearance of being materially poor that we feel obliged to refer to this. Even more so than in City, we were left with the impression of poverty.

We can hypothesize, on the basis of our work in City courts, that the social distance between judge and judged, which was present there also, need not produce either the 'objectification' of defendants or harsh juvenile justice. We would argue that City's operational rules, part of the court culture, honoured the safeguards of due process and restricted sentencing discretion, thus preventing social class prejudices and antagonisms spilling over into court proceedings. Such safeguards appeared less real in Countyside. Further, Countyside clerks and magistrates tend to make 'space' in the court proceedings for restructuring by inserting extraneous ideological and 'common sense' agendas about how justice should be administered.

An ideal way of disguising this insertion of a hidden agenda *vis-à-vis* administering justice is to claim, as many magistrates did in conversation with us, that 'each case is judged on its merits'. The dynamics of this operation are complex but we will be arguing in this (. . .) section that Countyside magistrates basically relied upon their own notions of adolescence, working-class family life, crime and its causes and the purpose of punishment. As a consequence of this, social class differentials, which as our analysis of City courts showed need not be influential, become so.

In this section we shall try to get over the obvious methodological difficulties of demonstrating the impact of social class on the administration of justice by using qualitative data taken from three sources. First, we had formal conversations with nearly all the magistrates who presided over observed sessions. That they happily met and talked with us, using the judgemental criteria we present below, is significant. Second, we draw on 'overheard' conversations between court officials, which took place during and after sessions, and between cases. Third, we draw on our own transcriptions of 'official' in-court discourse. We will deal with the impact of social distance by referring to issues of income, leisure and language.

First, we will consider Countyside officials' approach to matters relating to the income of poor people, the defendants and their parents. Fines in Countyside tend to be comparatively high and consistent with this was the magistrates' propensity to use compensation orders. In one case, which involved three boys convicted of stealing and joyriding a Daimler saloon, the juveniles were all sent to detention centre and banned from driving etc., but were also ordered to pay £200 compensation each. The compensation order was made in respect of repairs to the vehicle, although the court was aware that the bill had already been paid by the insurance company. One might wonder if the status of the car influenced this decision, not least because the presiding magistrates went out of their way to state, quite unsolicited, that the compensation had absolutely nothing at all to do with the car being a Daimler. Nor is it irrelevant to our analysis that when a juvenile sent to detention centre and ordered to pay £1,000 compensation (at £5 per week for four years) appealed to Crown Court against the sentence he had the compensation order quashed. It could be argued that sentencers, because of their cloistered social position, are unaware of the impact of demanding that an unemployed juvenile should pay over a third of his income for four years. There were occasions when this benign interpretation was given backing, in that magistrates would preface their sentence with suggestions of leniency:

We're *just* going to fine you £30 and £30 compensation.

Yet on occasions when parents offered to pay the whole sum of a fine there and then, rather than on weekly account, they clearly took court officials aback. On one occasion the clerk repeated the fine's amount slowly and said:

You're sure you can pay this sum in whole now, today?

Thus even the parent who responds to the formal sentence correctly, and without inviting social comment, receives it. Having so often and routinely quizzed defendants and parents about how much money they received each week, their hire purchase commitments, how much rent they paid and so on, court officials regarded relative affluence in a juvenile or his family almost as a form of defiance.

Countyside's officials displayed conservative attitudes towards leisure and the use of social space. Because they failed to consider leisure in the context of the lives of working-class adolescents, these attitudes proved judgemental and restrictive. Thus, in interrogating a boy as to what he does when not in school, a senior magistrate was told:

We play footie, go places, go to the cinema if I've got money.

The reply from the bench was crisp:

Ah! You muck around all day and con your mother.

Adolescents are often reprimanded by magistrates for being on the street at all. Window-shopping is implicitly forbidden. Anyone window-shopping must be up to no good. One magistrate went as far as to suggest a kind of unofficial curfew for adolescents hanging around the village part of the Countyside, with its proximity to the land of owner-occupied semi-detacheds:

It is a very serious thing to go wandering around the streets in Countyside village.

The use of complex language by court 'professionals' to 'cool out' defendants is well documented (Fears, 1977). We do not intend to dwell on this device here, except to say it was, as one would expect, a routine feature of Countyside court.

So far we have dealt with specific examples of stigmatization, which appear to be a product of the social-class distance between judge and judged. The clearest evidence that the social distance structurally present between judgers and judged affects court procedures concerns Countyside officials' development of a full-blown thesis about the nature of poor families and their 'criminal' way of life. Our fieldwork diaries became so laden with 'problem family' explanations that we were forced to identify this as a working model amongst court officials in Countyside. This model is basically pathological, corresponding in part with those explanations of social problems found in the 'culture of poverty' thesis. The central strand concerns the belief that Countyside is infested by an underclass of criminal families. We were sometimes briefed during proceedings when a reputed member of the criminal families brigade appeared. On one occasion we were passed a note:

One of our regulars. They are one of our oldest customers . . . his name is sprayed all over walls in the area.

These families, so the thesis goes, generally tend to be socially disordered. We note that clerks, perhaps unconsciously, confirmed this stereotyping in 'explaining' the sentencing decision to families, for instance by commenting in open court to a mother:

I think one of your other sons is going to the attendance centre for a similar offence.

And to a boy disposed of with a fine:

Perhaps, George, when your father comes out . . . er . . . comes out of prison, he'll help you pay.

Magistrates themselves expounded the criminal families thesis to us. One, for example, also a councillor, regarded them as nuisances and pollutants. He claimed to be pressurized by angry neighbours at his weekly surgeries, and favours a housing policy of moving them out, moving them on. In order to 'test' this thesis that there is a network of criminal families in Countyside, we analysed the names appearing on the juvenile court lists over the year during which we were observing. We found no evidence that such families existed as 'regular customers' of the juvenile court. When names did recur in the court, this was mainly the result of a series of remands. This might give an impression of recidivism but, certainly over the year's workload we analysed, there was no significant substantiation of the court officials' thesis. This particular ideological construction may stem from magistrates' other dealings with the local population as head teacher, councillor or employer. Whatever its source, it acts as a defence mechanism which can be utilized if the 'common-sense' principles court officials use in administering justice are ever challenged.

We have in this section relied heavily on extracts from official and unofficial discourse in and around the court to demonstrate our contention that the social-class position and subsequent cultural and ideological preferences of court officials spill over into the production of juvenile justice in Countyside court. (Parker *et al.*, 1981: 87–92)

Here is my summary of the main claims in Parker *et al.*'s argument:

1. In Countyside Court there was 'objectification of offenders' and punitive justice (pp. 87–8).
2. One possible reason for this was the sharp difference in the social-class backgrounds of magistrates and defendants (p. 88).
3. But this, in itself, is not a sufficient explanation since the same class differential was present at City Court, and justice there was less harsh. The crucial factor was deviations from the safeguards of due process and restricted sentencing discretion which allowed magistrates to insert 'extraneous ideological and "commonsense" agendas about how justice should be administered' (p. 88); agendas based on their own 'notions of adolescence, working-class family life, crime and its causes and the purposes of punishment' (p. 88). These notions were a product of their social-class background, as well as conservative in character and often inaccurate.

Summarising this account in terms of these three points obviously leaves a lot out, and some of this must be taken into account in any assessment of Parker *et al.*'s argument. Nonetheless, it seems to me that these are the *main* points made in this extract. Furthermore, they relate together in a coherent way, so that they can be read as forming a single overarching explanatory argument: Justice in Countyside Court is relatively punitive because the effects of the social-class differential between magistrates and defendants are not constrained by the operation of court procedures ensuring due process and restricted sentencing discretion.

It will not always be possible to find a coherent overall argument like this. In book-length accounts, especially, one may sometimes find a set of main points that relate to one another in a looser manner, perhaps only in the sense that they all concern the same case. More usually, though, there will be some stronger form of organisation. Clues to this may be found in the chapter titles. There are a number of common patterns in terms of which book-length ethnographic accounts may be organised. I mentioned one in Chapter 1 in connection with the Lynds' study of Middletown, each chapter covering a different aspect of community life. By contrast, sometimes the chapters follow a sequence of stages in some process that is of focal concern. For example, Rock's study of the prosecution of debtors includes the following chapter titles: 'Enforcement by creditors', 'The debt-collector', 'The solicitor', 'The county court', 'Execution' (of the summons), etc. (Rock, 1973). While the chapter headings of a research report themselves rarely indicate all of the main claims being made, they may well provide a framework in terms of which such claims can be organised.

It is worth noting that in identifying the main claims of an account one must be prepared to exercise some interpretative licence, since they may not be very clearly expressed. At the same time, though, one must ensure that the argument is not misrepresented. This is a matter of judgement, and sometimes different, but equally reasonable, versions may be possible.

Evidential claims

Much of what is left out of the summary of Parker *et al.*'s argument that I provided above consists of the evidence they offer in support of their major claims. This is clearly important and must be included in any detailed summary of the extract. Here, then, is an account of Parker *et al.*'s argument that includes both the main claims and the evidence presented to support them.[11]

1. In Countyside Court there was 'objectification' of offenders and punitive justice (p. 33 above).

    No evidence is presented directly in support of this claim in the extract, but some of the evidence used to establish the attitudes of magistrates might be interpreted as supporting it, such as the claim that fines tended to be high, the cases illustrating the use of compensation orders (p. 34), and the public reprimands of defendants (pp. 34–5).

2. One possible reason for the punitive treatment was the sharp difference in the social-class backgrounds of magistrates and defendants (p. 33).

The authors offer several arguments to support the claim that there was a social-class differential between magistrates and defendants in Countyside Court (p. 33):

(a) Published evidence about the middle-class and middle-aged character of magistrates in general.

(b) The fact that at Countyside magistrates frequently 'had to quit the bench abruptly for specific hearings because they knew defendants and their parents personally from acting as employer, head teacher, councillor and so on'.

(c) The argument that 'The magistrates were, in the main, professional and propertied people', while 'the defendants were, by and large, from one of the most deprived urban areas in the United Kingdom'.

(d) The claim that often 'defendants and parents (had) the appearance of being materially poor'.

3. The difference in social-class backgrounds is not, in itself, a sufficient explanation since this is also found at City Court. Particularly important at Countyside were deviations from the safeguards of due process and restricted sentencing discretion which allowed magistrates there to act on the basis of class-based, conservative and inaccurate assumptions.

A range of sorts of evidence is offered in support of this:

(a) The authors report that: 'safeguards appeared less real in Countyside' (p. 33).

(b) Information (general and specific) is provided about Countyside officials' attitude towards the income levels of defendants and their parents. It is reported that fines tend to be comparatively high (p. 34). Also, Countyside magistrates tend to use compensation orders:

    (i) A case is reported involving three boys: ordered to pay £200 compensation on top of a detention sentence and driving ban, even though repairs had already been paid for by the insurance company. The authors add:

> 'One might wonder if the status of the car influenced this decision, not least because the presiding magistrates went out of their way to state, quite unsolicited, that the compensation had absolutely nothing at all to do with the car being a Daimler'. (p. 34).

    (ii) Another case, this time of a juvenile sent to detention centre and ordered to pay £1,000 compensation (at £5 per week for four years). He appealed to the Crown Court against the sentence and the compensation order was quashed. The authors point out that this compensation represented 'over a third of his income for four years' (p. 34).

(iii) The authors offer what they call benign and less benign interpretations of these and other cases. The former is that the magistrates were unaware of the poverty of their defendants, hence the frequent comments by magistrates of the kind:

> we're *just* going to fine you £30 and £30 compensation. (p.34).

However, they also report contrary evidence which suggests the less benign interpretation that the magistrates intended the treatment to be harsh. They report that court officials showed shock when parents offered to pay fines in full. They comment on this:

> Thus even the parent who responds to the formal sentence correctly, and without inviting social comment, receives it. Having so often routinely quizzed defendants and parents about how much money they received each week, their hire purchase commitments, how much rent they paid and so on, court officials regarded relative affluence in a juvenile or his family almost as a form of defiance. (p. 34)

(c) The authors also report that Countyside's officials displayed conservative attitudes towards leisure and the use of social space. (p. 34)

(i) A case is cited of a magistrate interrogating a boy about what he does when not in school, receiving the reply

> We play footie, go places, go to the cinema if I've got money,

and commenting

> Ah! You muck around all day and con your mother. (p. 34)

(ii) Adolescents were often reprimanded by magistrates for being on the street at all:

> Anyone window-shopping must be up to no good. One magistrate went as far as to suggest a kind of unofficial curfew for adolescents hanging around the village part of Countyside, with its proximity to the land of owner-occupied semi-detacheds: 'It is a very serious thing to go wandering around the streets in Countyside village.' (p. 35)

(d) It is also claimed that court officials routinely used complex language to 'cool out' defendants. The only evidence relevant to this is a published source: Fears (1977).

(e) The authors report that 'The clearest evidence that the social distance structurally present between judgers and judged affects court procedures concerns Countyside officials' development of a full-blown thesis about the nature of poor families and their 'criminal' way of life'. They report that their fieldwork diaries became laden with '"problem family" explanations' (p. 35). This criminal family thesis operated as a working model, and had as its central assumption that Countryside is infested by an underclass of criminal families.

> One one occasion we were passed a note: 'One of our regulars. They are one of our oldest customers . . . his name is sprayed all over walls in the area.' (p. 91)

These families were viewed as socially disordered. Clerks confirmed this stereotyping in explaining sentencing to families. To a mother in open court:

> I think one of your other sons is going to the attendance centre for a similar offence. (p. 35)

> To a boy given a fine: Perhaps, George, when your father comes out . . . er . . . comes out of prison, he'll help you pay. (p. 35)

The criminal families thesis was expounded in interviews with the researchers.

> One, (magistrate) (. . .), also a councillor, regarded them as nuisances and pollutants (p. 35).

The authors argue that the criminal families thesis is false:

> In order to 'test' this thesis that there is a network of criminal families in Countyside, we analysed the names appearing on the juvenile court lists over the year during which we were observing. We found no evidence that such families existed as 'regular customers' of the juvenile court. (p. 35)

This is not the only way in which Parker *et al.*'s evidence may be summarised, but I think it broadly captures the structure of their argument. In looking at the evidence listed here we should note that it is not all of a piece. Sometimes a claim stands on its own, sometimes it is supported by evidence, and sometimes that evidence is itself supported by further evidence. (I have tried to indicate something of this structure by indenting supporting arguments.)

Whether looking at main arguments or at evidence we must pay attention to the *types* of claim involved. In the next section I shall look in more detail at these types.

Types of claim

There seem to me to be six sorts of argument typically found in ethnographic accounts (as main and/or as evidential claims). These can be listed under three headings[12]:

1. Definitions.
2. Factual claims
   (a) descriptions
   (b) explanations
   (c) predictions.
3. Value claims
   (a) evaluations
   (b) prescriptions.

1. *Definitions.* Definitions tell us how a particular term is being used in an account. For instance, in introducing a distinction between teaching and survival strategies on the part of secondary school teachers, Woods provides the following definition of 'survival':

(. . .) It is, in short, a *survival* problem. What is at risk is not only (the teacher's) physical, mental and nervous safety and well-being, but also his continuance in professional life, his future prospects, his professional identity, his way of life, his status, his self-esteem (. . .). (Woods, 1979a: 145)

Woods is spelling out here what he means when he claims that teachers are concerned with 'survival'. And he also defines 'teaching', (adopting the definition put forward by the philosopher Paul Hirst) as 'activity intended to bring about learning' (Hirst, 1971).

It is very unlikely that the major claims of an ethnographic study would be definitional. However, definitions may well form a part of the substructure of the argument. Also, we would not expect to find evidence offered in support of definitions, though reasons indicating their appropriateness may be provided.[13]

2. *Factual claims.* By factual claims I mean those that document features of the case studied by the ethnographer, and/or their causes and consequences. These claims may take several forms: descriptions, explanations, or predictions.

(a) DESCRIPTIONS. Descriptions are one of the most important sorts of argument to be found in ethnographic texts, since all of the other types of argument (apart from definitions) depend on them. We cannot explain, predict, evaluate, prescribe or theorise about something without describing it, or at least assuming some description of it.

What I mean by a description is a verbal representation of some feature of a scene. In the course of their account of justice at Countyside Parker *et al.* present many descriptions. Indeed, one of their main claims in the extract quoted is a description: that Countyside justice is punitive.[14] What is being suggested here is that the same sorts of case receive more severe punishments at Countyside than they would elsewhere. The authors also provide descriptions as evidence. Thus, in seeking to illustrate the effects of the social-class background of magistrates on Countyside justice, they describe court officials as displaying 'conservative attitudes towards leisure and the use of social space', and support this with further descriptive evidence in the form of two illustrative cases.

As I noted earlier, the naturalistic mode of writing tends to present descriptions as if they simply reproduced the phenomena described. Yet, they do not; they are always selective. We can always provide a very large number of mutually compatible descriptions of the same scene. Descriptions represent phenomena from particular points of view that are designed to serve certain purposes, for example to provide evidence for other claims. So, in identifying descriptions, we need to pay attention to the function they are intended to serve. In large part this is a matter of noting how they fit into the argumentative structure of the account and how they relate to the research focus.

As an illustration of the selective character of descriptions, take the following brief description from Parker *et al.*: '(A clerk commented) in open court to a woman "I think one of your other sons is going to the attendance centre for a similar offence"' p. 35 above. We can see how not just the content of the utterance but also the fact that it was to the mother of the defendant, and that it was made in open court, are relevant: because the description is intended to illustrate the stereotyping of offenders and their families as belonging to a criminal underclass. The implication is, I think, that such utterances not only reflect but also publicly reinforce court personnel's stereotypes. At the same time, though, it seems certain that there were many other features of that comment and its surrounding context which could have been mentioned, but which were judged irrelevant. For example, we are not told anything about the woman other than that she was a mother who had more than two sons, two being currently or recently defendants, one of whom was being sent to an attendance centre. We are told nothing about the clerk beyond the fact that he/she was a clerk. We are given the words spoken, but not told anything about tone of voice, facial expression, etc., on the part of the clerk or of the woman's (or others') reactions to what was said. Nor do we know anything about what had happened before or after this comment was made (other than that the court was in process). The information that could have been included in this description is virtually endless, and the same is true with all descriptions. Writers must select and include what they take to be relevant, and leave out the rest. As readers, though, we must bear in mind that this process of selection has occurred, since in assessing validity we may need to consider the reasonableness of the judgements about what was and was not treated as relevant.

There is another aspect of the selective character of descriptions that needs attention. We should note how a description like the one discussed above can itself be categorised in a variety of ways. The authors present the comment by the clerk as an instance of stereotyping on the part of court personnel, portraying the families of defendants as 'socially disordered'. However, we could treat it as many other things: as an example of talk in a relatively public setting, as an instance of male–female or of female–female talk (depending on the sex of the clerk), as (perhaps) an interchange between an older and a younger person, as an utterance indicating what was probably spurious uncertainty (it seems unlikely that the clerk was actually uncertain about the verdict on the other son) etc. Here again, there is a wide range of possibilities; and the more detail there is in the original description, usually, the more alternative higher level descriptions are possible. As we shall see in Chapter 5, when it comes to assessing the validity of descriptions, we must bear in mind the possible relevance of both what has been left out of descriptions and of alternative interpretations of the evidence presented.

Another aspect of descriptions that must be given attention is the distinction between those dealing with singular events and generalisations. The claim about Countyside court officials displaying conservative attitudes towards leisure is a generalisation about what many of them did on many occasions (it is a generalisation across magistrates and over time). By contrast, the description of a magistrate 'interrogating a boy about what he does when not in school' (p. 90) is a singular description. As we shall see in Chapter 4, generalisations require additional evidence over and above what is required to support singular descriptions.

(b) EXPLANATIONS. Where descriptions provide an account of features of some phenomenon, explanations are concerned with *why* one or more of those features occurred and seek to show that they are the product of particular factors within temporal and spatial striking distance (direct or indirect). Take Rist's study of the teacher–pupil interaction in the early years of schooling. It is the central claim of his account that the differential school achievement of the children is in large part a product of the teachers' social class-based expectations of them. So in this study, besides providing descriptions of the teachers' procedures for allocating children to groups and of their interaction with members of these groups, Rist also makes an explanatory claim. Indeed, the descriptive claims are subordinated to the task of explanation; much as they are in the extract from Parker *et al.*, where the overall argument is concerned with explaining why justice at Countyside is relatively punitive.

Explanations may also operate in a subordinate role in ethnographic accounts. Thus, at one point in his study of medical students' experience of the clinical years of their course, Atkinson refers to the well-known phenomenon of "'medical students' disease" – that is, the hypochondria to which medical students are prone' (Atkinson, 1981a: 21). He notes that this has been explained by others in terms of the stress and anxiety produced by extreme academic pressure, but he puts forward a different explanation: that it results from 'a heightened awareness of the clinical', indeed an 'absorption' in clinical matters:

Students became more or less adept at handling a complex symbolic domain in which disease categories and diagnostic inference figure pre-eminently. It should therefore come as little surprise that clinical understanding should come to occupy a dominant position in the students' repertoire of conceptual schemes. (pp. 21–2)

What he is suggesting is that students' very familiarity with clinical interpretations leads them to apply these to things that others would interpret differently. This argument is not a major claim of Atkinson's study, but rather offers further support for his descriptive argument that in the clinical years of their course the students become 'absorbed, seduced almost, by the clinical gaze' (p. 22).

It is in the nature of explanations that they rely on theoretical assumptions. Thus, Atkinson's explanation for medical students' hypochondria relies on the theoretical idea that when people are learning a new mode of interpretation there will be a tendency for them to 'over-use' it, applying it to circumstances that others would treat differently. If we did not find this assumption plausible, then we could not judge Atkinson's explanation persuasive (unless it were supported by some other plausible theoretical assumption). As we shall see, assessing the theoretical assumptions built into explanations is an important step in judging their validity. So, in identifying explanations, we need to look out for the theoretical assumptions that they presuppose.

Explanations, like descriptions, are also based on relevances.[15] For any phenomenon, we can identify a potentially infinite number of causes. There may be one or more immediate causes, and each of these can in turn be explained in terms of other causes, and so on, *ad infinitum*. Which (or which combination) of these we select will depend on how the explanation fits into the overall argument and its relation to the research focus. For instance, we may explain the differential performance of the children that Rist studied in terms of differences in academic ability or in their attitude to school. And each of these (along with Rist's own preferred explanatory factor, the teachers' expectations) could be explained on the basis of more remote factors, for example differences in the children's home background.

Furthermore, the latter could, in turn, be explained by appeal to family histories, and/or to the nature of the local communities from which the children come. And these, again, may be accounted for on the basis of various features of the character and history of US society, notably its racial and class structure. And so on. The implication of this is that where explanations are presented we must look out for any indication of the relevances that have guided the selection of explanatory factors.

(c) PREDICTIONS. By predictions I mean claims that if particular conditions are met, other events will occur. Here is an example, again from Parker *et al.*'s study of juvenile courts:

It seems quite clear that whilst sifting and prosecution decision-making remain in the hands of the police who are given no clear guidelines about how such a process should operate, that the 'push-in' tendency (that is, the tendency to prosecute most offences rather than using 'no further action' or an on-the-spot warning) is likely to dominate. This dominance is almost assured when local decision-making rests with front-line urban policemen. (Parker *et al.*, 1981: 42–3)

It is being predicted here that as long as it is the police who make the decision about whether to pursue charges the 'push-in' tendency will continue (and, by implication, that if others made the decision the push-in tendency would diminish).

Predictions are symmetrical with explanations. Where in explaining something we start with what happened and look for significant causes, in predicting we start with some actual or possible state of affairs and pick out effects that are significant. Once again, relevances underly the process of analysis here. There is an infinite number of potential consequences that may follow from any given conditions. Which ones are picked out will depend in part on which seem most likely; but equally important will be the significance of these various consequences. In the case of Parker *et al.*'s prediction, for example, it seems likely that (besides the consequence they identify) the fact that it is the police who decide whether offenders will or will not be prosecuted means that there will be more work for the police and less for lawyers, and perhaps also that decisions will be made more rapidly than they might otherwise be, etc. The authors pick out the 'push-in' effect because it is of great significance given their focus on the fairness of the administration of justice.

Predictions are relatively uncommon in ethnographic research, and rarely form part of the major claims. They do occur occasionally however. As with explanations, when we identify predictive claims we must look out for the theoretical claims implicit in them, and for the relevances that have structured them.

3. *Value claims.* By value claims I mean those which not only

describe, explain and/or make predictions about a feature but also express some view about it in terms of one or more values.

(a) EVALUATIONS. Evaluations involve a description of and perhaps also explanation for a set of phenomena *plus* some indication that the thing described or explained is good or bad. Much ethnography openly shuns evaluative intent, being concerned with describing what *is* rather than what *ought to be*.[16] However, ethnographic methods are increasingly being used in research that is labelled as evaluative (Fetterman, 1984; Fetterman and Pitman, 1986). And it is not uncommon to find evaluative claims embedded in conventional ethnographic accounts. For example, in Peter Woods' description of the process of course choice at the secondary school he studied, at one point he contests the teachers' claim that 'the advice and guidance offered is given in the best interests of the pupil' (Woods, 1979a: 51). Here he is moving beyond description and explanation to an evaluation of the teachers' actions (Hammersley, 1990b). In much the same way, in their study of an industrial unit for slow learners, Atkinson *et al.* make several evaluative claims. For example, they comment:

For the most part, it is not at all clear that the students' skills are significantly changed, in terms of their competence with industrial machinery. There is little or no sense of their progressing through graded tasks, and of measurable improvement in performance. (Atkinson *et al.*, 1981 :255)

Here, the terms 'significantly' and 'improvement', and perhaps others, indicate evaluative intent.

Evaluations necessarily imply some set of values, and we need to be on the look-out for information about what these are. However, as a result of the fact that evaluations are often regarded as inappropriate in ethnographic accounts, the value assumptions on which they are based may not be explicit.

Parker *et al.*'s book on juvenile courts is an example of an ethnographic study where the overall argument is explicitly value-based. In the first chapter they present their research as an evaluation of two local juvenile courts in the Merseyside area. The evaluation is in terms of justice, an important element of this being the consistency of each court in its treatment of similar cases, and consistency between different courts. Following their account of Countyside Court which I quoted at some length earlier, they examine the Court's treatment of car offences and then conclude:

The punitive nature of the disposals *vis-à-vis* car offences is in itself important, but just as significant is the way in which this policy illustrates the inconsistency, and thus lack of rational sentencing policy, which is both created by, and reinforces, the administration of justice via class antagonism. (Parker *et al.*, 1981: 92)

'Punitive' seems likely to be an evaluative as well as a descriptive term in this context, as also are 'inconsistency' and 'rational'. Parker *et al.* provide us with some information about the values underlying their evaluation in a concluding chapter, where they distinguish between natural and social justice, the latter involving consideration of the social conditions in which people live in deciding what is a just punishment.

(b) PRESCRIPTIONS. Occasionally, on the basis of their research, ethnographers outline some recommendations about what changes ought to be made in the phenomena they have studied. For example, in the final chapter of his book *The Ceremonial Order of the Clinic*, Strong outlines a number of practical recommendations for the conduct of paediatric consultations that arise from his research. Thus, he suggests that the presence of students at consultations led to patients getting less time and less privacy, and is not a very satisfactory form of teaching either (Strong, 1979: 20). Sometimes prescriptions are less clearly signalled than this. In the conclusion to an account of 'the coping strategies that teachers use to deal with the constraints imposed upon them by the British educational system', Andy Hargreaves offers the following:

> The crucial axis which might provide the possibility for radical alteration and humanisation of our educational and social structures would seem to be that which connects teacher 'experience' to structural constraints. Change of such a magnitude demands the active involvement of teachers in particular, and men and women in general, in the collective criticism of existing practices, structural arrangements and institutional goals. Furthermore, the possibility of change is contingent upon the provision of institutional conditions under which such collective criticism could take place and be reflexively integrated with ongoing practice. Paradoxically, this requires the fulfillment of 'gradualist' policies such as small class-sizes and the creation of more 'free-time' so that a meaningful integration between theory and practice might arise and thus produce a reconstruction of teacher 'experience' on radical lines, infusing it with the power of transformation. (Hargreaves, 1984: 81–3)

What is being suggested here is not very clearly specified, and it is worth noting that Hargreaves does not explicitly recommend the possible 'radical alteration and humanisation' he mentions, but it seems obvious that he is nonetheless to be read as prescribing it.

The critical reader needs to be on the look-out for evaluations and prescriptions that seem to take the form of descriptions, explanations or predictions. And, as with evaluations, in trying to understand prescriptions we must look out for explications of the values underlying them.

5. IDENTIFYING CONCLUSIONS

Earlier, I drew a distinction between major claims and conclusions, the former applying to the case, the latter going beyond it to deal with the focus of the study (where this is more general than the case). There are two ways in which this may be done: by drawing a theoretical conclusion (what I shall call 'theoretical inference') or by generalising the findings in the case studied to a larger population of cases ('empirical generalisation').

Theoretical inference

As we saw, it is common for ethnographers to conceive of their goal as the production of theoretical descriptions. These are believed simultaneously to describe and explain the phenomena to which they refer, as well as accounting for other phenomena of the same type (and thereby offering a theory). In my view, such different tasks cannot be achieved by the same means; they place quite divergent requirements on the researcher (Hammersley, 1990c). Indeed, I believe that many of the weaknesses of ethnographic accounts stem from the failure to recognise this. By pursuing a composite set of goals, ethnographers often achieve none of them very effectively. Probably the most important distinction to be made here is between a primary focus on the particular and a concern with the universal. Both descriptions and explanations refer to particular phenomena occurring in particular places at particular times. So too do empirical generalisations (though it will be many places and/or many times). Theories, on the other hand, are concerned with why one type of phenomenon tends to produce another (other things being equal) *wherever* instances of that type occur. (This universality is, of course, what gives theories their potential relevance to a wide audience.) While studies concerned with theoretical claims do, of course, have an interest in particular phenomena, that interest is limited to the relevance of those phenomena for developing and testing the theoretical claim.

There are also some difficult questions about the nature of theory in the social sciences. As I noted in Chapter 1, a nineteenth-century positivist view of the nature of laws informed some early ethnographic work, both anthropological and sociological. From this point of view, laws identify regular, causal connections between types of phenomena to be found wherever such phenomena occur, and these laws can be precisely formulated and their operation demonstrated. The model here was the laws of Newtonian physics. This conception of law was used by defenders of the case study method to deny claims that the statistical method represented the scientific study of the social world. It was argued that since that method could only produce probabilistic generalisations it did not generate laws and therefore was not scientific. This argument has been largely abandoned by ethnographers today, along with the commitment to the discovery of sociological laws. But little attention has been given by them to alternative conceptions of theory. This problem remains unresolved and all we can do for the moment is bear the issue in mind when dealing with the theoretical claims that ethnographers make.[17]

It is rather rare to find ethnographic research explicitly and single-mindedly pursuing theory. There are only a few examples, notably Lindesmith's study of opiate addiction and Cressey's work on embezzlement (Lindesmith, 1937 and 1968; Cressey, 1950 and 1953). Most present-day ethnography is primarily concerned with description and explanation. However, broader theoretical claims are often made on the basis of these descriptions and explanations, and these should be noted (along with any indication of the basis on which the link between claims and theoretical conclusion is being made).

A fairly typical example of the sorts of theoretical claim made, and the kind of basis outlined for them, is provided by Woods in his study of subject choice processes in secondary schools. He argues that some schools in the English education system are more 'constrained' than others, and that the school he studied had an 'extra burden':

it was about to become a comprehensive, not uncontentiously in the area at large. This introduced extra problems of validation, for it was considered imperative by senior staff at the school that it be seen as 'working' by parents of erstwhile grammar school children. The traditional symbol of worthiness is examination results. A common device to 'improve' these is to present them in the form of percentages – that is, as proportions of those taking the examinations. (. . .) Clearly, all this throws the utmost importance onto one's selection processes. And since most examination courses begin in the fourth year, it would appear that third year subject choice, wherein pupils 'choose' the courses they wish to pursue for the next two years, is of crucial importance. (Woods, 1979b: 171–2)

What Woods is suggesting here is a theory that pressure on schools for 'good' examination results reduces the degree of choice that they give to pupils as regards fourth- and fifth-year courses. From this point of view Lowfield, the school he studied, might be regarded as a critical case because there (it is claimed) the theoretical variable (examination pressure) is at a high level compared to other schools. To the extent that this is true, we can draw conclusions about the validity of the theory from information about what happened at Lowfield.

Empirical generalisation

Instead of using the ethnographic case study as a basis for theoretical conclusions, ethnographers may alternatively seek to generalise from it to an aggregate of cases that is of general interest. As I noted earlier, while relatively few people may be interested in what life was like in Winston Street, Washington DC, in the 1960s, many more are probably interested in, say, the nature of black ghetto life in the second half of the twentieth century. Thus, Hannerz effectively uses his study of a case that is of rather limited interest in itself as a basis for generalisation to a whole that is of much wider interest. This is a very common strategy used by ethnographers.

However, ethnographers are often not very clear about the nature of the whole to which they are generalising. An example is Punch's study of policing in Amsterdam's Warmoesstraat. As we saw, he justifies his study of this case on the grounds that previous studies of the police have not taken account of the full range of conditions under which policing takes place, since there has been little investigation of police work in large 'cosmopolitan' city centres. Two questions arise from this. First, what population of metropolitan inner-cities is Punch seeking to generalise to on the basis of his research on the Warmoesstraat? Second, to the extent that this is intended to contribute to our knowledge of some larger picture of police practice, what are the boundaries of that picture? Punch does not answer either of these questions very clearly, but presumably the answer to the latter (in broad terms) is that he is seeking to generalise about policing in Western societies in the late twentieth century.

Identifying the basis for conclusions

Ethnographers are also often not clear about whether they are using theoretical inference or empirical generalisation to link their findings to their conclusions about the focus of the research. Often, appeals to both strategies are made. Punch's study illustrates this. While in some places he seems to be concerned with drawing empirical generalisations from his findings, elsewhere he appears to draw theoretical conclusions. Thus, in the final chapter of his book, he claims that:

The relevance of this case study is that it sets out to examine the role that patrolmen play in the social life of the inner city with the intention of illuminating some of the micro-processes which contribute to a more general analysis of the nature and quality of social order in such an environment. (Punch, 1979: 179)

This could be interpreted as hinting at a theory about the social conditions that produce different types of social order and disorder.

Westley's study of *Violence and the Police* provides another example where both theoretical inference and empirical generalisation seem to be involved, but here it is possible to identify the two more clearly:

> The purpose of this study was not to describe the urban police departments of the United States but to articulate the ways in which the occupation and technology of policing gave rise to a set of shared human responses – in the form of attitudes and values. Insofar as we were successful in identifying some of the major components and problems of policing as an occupation and analyzing how these gave rise to police norms, the results should be applicable wherever these conditions hold. Obviously, they don't hold for all police departments. Some police departments were at that time so corrupt that there was almost no professional core to their activities, and 'our' department certainly did not represent them. Other departments were so highly professionalized and controlled by civil service regulations that most of the attitudes we described never developed. (. . .) But between these two poles of high professionalization and widespread corruption we should guess that most of the major urban police departments in the United States would be found. We should argue that to the degree that any police department was faced with the conditions of public hostility, public pressure, political influence, and opportunities for graft, they would probably respond with the normative system analogous to that described in this book. That many police departments held the same view of their work and of the public was at least partially demonstrated when a California newspaper posed our questions on secrecy to men from seven different departments in the San Francisco area and received almost identical responses. (Westley, 1970: xii)

Here the primary basis for drawing conclusions seems to be theoretical inference. But the question of how far the conditions specified in the theory hold in various US police departments is also addressed.

In examining the conclusions drawn in ethnographic studies, then, we need to be attuned to whether theoretical inference or empirical generalisation, or both, are involved. In the case of theoretical conclusions we need to be clear about the theory the case(s) have been used to develop and/or test and about why they are believed to provide the basis for theoretical inference. Where empirical generalisation is involved, we must look out for indications of the larger whole to which generalisation is being made, and for the reasons why such generalisation is believed to be sound.

CONCLUSION

In this chapter I have examined the task of understanding ethnographic accounts. I have emphasised that understanding texts is not a straightforward business, the meaning is not there on the page for us to pick up. We must work at making sense of what the author is telling us and why. And we should not take her or his own statements about the message as beyond revision. Authors are not always as clear and consistent as they might be and we must look at the claims they actually make, as well as those that they claim to make.

I identified several aspects of ethnographic accounts that we should look out for: the focus; the case(s) studied; the methods used; the main claims and evidence; and, finally, any conclusions that are drawn.

Developing a summary account of an ethnographic text which covers these various elements provides us with a basis for the next step of our task: making an assessment of that account. But before we can do this, we must consider the question of the criteria by which such assessment should be made. This is the task of the next chapter.

NOTES

1. Brown (1977); Atkinson (1982); Marcus and Cushman (1982); Hammersley and Atkinson (1983); Edmondson (1984); Clifford and Marcus (1986); Marcus and Fischer (1986); Geertz (1988); van Maanen (1988); Clifford (1988); Atkinson (1990).
2. I shall use the these terms interchangeably. As might be expected, there is a close link between the commitment to naturalism on the part of ethnographers that I outlined in Chapter 1 and use of the naturalistic mode of presentation.
3. It is worth noting that experiments in ethnographic writing are not new. Bateson's *Naven* is a precursor of some of the more recent developments (Bateson, 1958). And the use of life histories is, of course, by no means novel in anthropology or sociology. See Radin (1926), Shaw (1930), Lewis (1961, 1964 and 1970), and Klockars (1974) for examples. Gottschalk (1945), Dollard (1971) and Plummer (1983) provide useful methodological discussions of life history research.
4. See Hammersley (1990c).
5. I shall look briefly at assessing the research process itself in Chapter 7.
6. I shall provide more detail about these distinctions later.
7. This rationale illustrates the point I made in Chapter 1 about the balancing act that ethnographers often perform, maintaining distance both from science (or at least from quantitative research) on the one hand, and from literature on the other.
8. See Spradley (1979) for discussion of the range that ethnographic questions can take.
9. It is common to refer to the main claims of a study as its findings. I shall use this term on occasions myself, as here, but it is worth noting that it is potentially misleading. It may be taken to suggest that the researcher had little role in the research, that he or she merely *found* certain things to be the case. This usage matches the questionable assumptions of ethnographic naturalism.
10. Since this is a relatively brief extract from one chapter of a book,

its argument depends, partly, on material to be found elsewhere. However, it will serve for the purposes of illustration.

11. In fact, the authors do not present evidence specifically in relation to the distinct components of their argument, but seek to support it as a whole. I have allocated the evidence to each of the claims as seems most appropriate. Also, note that I am not concerned here with the quality or validity of this evidence. I shall look at this question in Chapter 5.

12. These correspond broadly to the types of product mentioned in the earlier discussion of research focus. I have omitted empirical generalisation and theoretical inference from the list since these are usually conclusions rather than claims.

13. It is worth noting that if examples are used to establish a definition they could legitimately be fictional, since they are intended only to illustrate usage.

14. This claim is ambiguous; it may also be interpreted as an evaluation. For the moment I shall deal with it as description.

15. For a useful discussion of this point, see Hart and Honoré (1985), Part I, Section I, philosophical preliminaries.

16. For the argument that this is as it should be, see, for example, Wolcott (1982).

17. For a detailed discussion of this problem, see Hammersley (1989a).

Criteria for assessing ethnographic research

The question of the criteria in terms of which ethnographic studies should be assessed is the point at which disagreements about the nature of ethnography are most sharply focused. It penetrates to the heart of the relationship between ethnography and quantitative research, and between both of these and the methods of natural science. Ethnographers are themselves divided on this issue. Some believe that the criteria that are normally applied to quantitative research are also appropriate for qualitative research. Others argue for criteria that are distinctive to ethnography. I shall look at each of these approaches, before outlining my own views about this issue.

There is by no means complete and clear agreement among quantitative researchers about the criteria in terms of which their research should be addressed. However, there are two sets of concepts that are commonly used to guide such assessment. The most comprehensive is the distinction between internal and external validity (Campbell, 1957; Campbell and Stanley, 1963; Cook and Campbell, 1979). This distinction was developed in the context of experimental and quasi-experimental research, and in particular the experimentalist's characteristic concern with hypothesis-testing and how research can be designed so as to rule out various types of threat to validity. There is some ambiguity in the use of these terms, but (broadly speaking): 'internal validity' refers to whether (within a particular experiment) the treatment administered actually caused the predicted outcome; 'external validity' refers to whether this causal relationship can be generalised to other cases. There have been several attempts to apply this scheme to ethnographic research (Denzin, 1978; Evans, 1983; LeCompte and Goetz, 1982; Goetz and LeCompte, 1984).

In my view, the very basis of this distinction is unsound, since it assumes that the issue of whether a causal relationship has been discovered in the experiment is separate from the question of whether it occurs elsewhere. Yet, to claim that a causal relationship has been found in one case is necessarily to imply that a similar relationship will be found in other cases of the same type. The very concept of cause implies a relationship that always (or probabilistically) occurs when certain conditions are met; and therefore it cannot refer to a single case alone.[1] From this point of view, there is only one form of validity, not two. Campbell identifies a variety of types of threat to validity on the basis of the distinction between internal and external validity, and this discussion is of considerable value. However, the distinction itself is misleading (Hammersley, 1991).

The other scheme in terms of which quantitative research is frequently assessed is framed by the concepts of reliability and validity. On most interpretations, this is less comprehensive than the distinction between internal and external validity, focusing primarily on measurement. Generally speaking, 'validity' refers to accuracy of measurement, 'reliability' to consistency of measurement. There have been several attempts to apply these concepts to ethnographic research (Denzin, 1978; Evans, 1983; Dobbert, 1984; LeCompte and Goetz, 1982; Goetz and LeCompte, 1984; Kirk and Miller, 1986).

Here again, there are conceptual problems. In large part these stem from the confusingly diverse ways in which the terms 'validity' and 'reliability' are used. There is divergence, for instance, about whether they refer to properties of measurement instruments, of observers, or of particular measurements; and over whether they are defined by the relationship between findings and the properties being measured, or in terms of a relationship among findings produced by different measurement instruments (Hammersley, 1987a). At the very least, some conceptual clarification is required. Furthermore, the restriction of the focus to measurement means that, in its normal form, this scheme cannot provide a sufficient set of criteria, even for the assessment of quantitative studies.

In short, while these quantitative concepts identify important considerations in the assessment of research, they do not provide a clear and coherent, or sufficient, conceptual basis for such assessment.

The argument that there are distinctive criteria for judging ethnographic research usually draws on one or more of the three methodological assumptions (naturalism, understanding and discovery) that I outlined in Chapter 1. Thus, the commitment to naturalism is sometimes taken to imply that the sole assessment criterion should be whether the account accurately captures the phenomenon being described. This view can take at least two forms. The phenomenon may be defined as the perspectives of the people under study. Here the aim of ethnography is to map the perceptions and interpretations of participants, and perhaps also to document the cultural resources by which these were produced. More commonly, the phenomenon being described goes beyond participants' understandings and includes their behaviour and the wider context. On both interpretations, though, the appropriate criterion of assessment is the extent to which the people's perspectives and/or behaviour and context are accurately represented.

The influence of naturalism and of the other two assumptions can be seen in some of the distinctive criteria that have been proposed for ethnographic research, but there are other influences too (such as an emphasis on theory development).[2] Here is a composite list of criteria that have been recommended as distinctive to ethnography by a number of writers (Frake, 1962; Lofland, 1974; Wolcott, 1975; Owens, 1982; Miles and Huberman, 1984; Athens, 1984; Lincoln and Guba, 1985):

1. the degree to which substantive and formal theory are produced and the degree of development of the theory;[3]
2. the novelty of the claims made;
3. the consistency of the claims with empirical observations;
4. the credibility of the account to readers and/or to those studied;
5. the extent to which the cultural description produced provides a basis for competent performance in the culture studied;
6. the extent to which the findings are transferable to other settings;
7. the reflexivity of the account: the degree to which the effects of research strategies on the findings are assessed and/or the amount of information about the research process that is provided to readers.

There is much to be learned from these criteria, but in my view (once again) they are not acceptable as they stand. For instance, the first applies only to research that is concerned with producing theory. It could not be a general criterion, unless we were to insist that all ethnography be directed towards producing theory, and there seems no good reason to do so. Another problem is that several of the criteria (notably the third, fourth, fifth and seventh) refer to *means* of assessment rather than to a *standard* in terms of which assessment should be made.[4] Finally, it is questionable whether these criteria are specific to ethnography. In my view, to the extent that they capture important issues they are equally applicable to quantitative research.

The two approaches to the problem of criteria that I have outlined above differ primarily in terms of whether they treat ethnography as sharing broadly the same methodological framework as quantitative research or as based on quite different methodological assumptions. Adopting the first approach the task becomes applying (and perhaps modifying) the criteria used by quantitative researchers to ethnography. The second approach has generally taken the form of seeking to identify the criteria actually used by ethnographers. But, as I have suggested, neither approach is satisfactory as it stands, and in part this stems from a failure to address the most important question that needs to be asked before we can decide on criteria: what is research for, what function should it be designed to serve? In my view its function is, put baldly, to produce *knowledge* that is of public *relevance*. This goal, and the criteria that derive from it, apply as much to ethnography as to other sorts of social research. While this perspective incorporates many of the ideas to be found in the two approaches I have discussed, unlike them it provides a coherent and comprehensive framework for assessing the value of research: in terms of the twin standards of validity and relevance. In discussing these criteria I shall fill in more detail about the view of social research on which they are based. And, as we shall see, straightforward as it may seem, this definition of the function of social research is not without difficulties or beyond dispute.

VALIDITY

By 'validity' I mean truth: interpreted as the extent to which an account accurately represents the social phenomena to which it refers. There are few concepts that have led to more controversy among philosophers than this one. Indeed, there are many social scientists, including ethnographers, who reject it as inapplicable to their work. As we saw in Chapter 1, there are critics of ethnography who, on the grounds that its procedures are unscientific, question that its findings can have validity. Equally, there are those who argue that ethnographers' claims to represent the social world are false because no such representation is ever possible.

In the first chapter I discussed a number of grounds on which ethnographic research is sometimes dismissed as unscientific. I want to concentrate here on one that is especially important in the context of the assessment of research findings. A common view of the process of assessment as it occurs in the natural sciences (and by extension in the social sciences) is what we might call the replication model. Here, fellow scientists read research reports and set about replicating the experiments described to discover whether the same results are produced. If they are, the claims made by the original researchers are accepted into the body of scientific knowledge; if the results are not reproduced, then the original researcher's claims are rejected as spurious.

However, there are severe limits on the possibility and practice of replication in the social sciences, and especially in ethnography. This is not just because of ethical limitations concerning the use of experiments on human beings, but also because (even within experiments) people's behaviour cannot be controlled to the same degree as can that of other animals and of inanimate objects. And, indeed, in ethnographic research such control is not even attempted. Instead, the aim is the investigation of 'naturally occurring' behaviour, and this requires the researcher to minimise her/his impact on what is observed. For these reasons replication is difficult, if not impossible, in ethnographic research. Restudies of the same setting are sometimes carried out but they often focus on different aspects of the setting, may use other research strategies, and have to take account of changes in the setting over the intervening time.

Given the problems involved in attempts to replicate ethnographic studies, and the rarity of such attempts, it might be concluded that there is no possibility of rigorous assessment of their findings. However, this would be a mistaken conclusion to draw. This is both because while replications do take place in the natural sciences they are less straightforward than the replication model implies, and because replication is not synonymous with rigorous assessment:

1. It is not always clear when replication of an experiment has or has not been achieved, or what it requires. Complete information about experimental procedure can never be provided, and it is not always clear what sorts of variation should and should not affect the outcome of the experiment (Collins, 1975).[5]

2. The results of a replication are not as easy to interpret as the model implies. There are reasons why the claims may still be true even though the replication failed to produce the same results, and vice versa. This is because scientists rely on theoretical assumptions in interpreting the findings of the original study and those of any replication. As a result, both are open to potentially conflicting interpretations.

3. Replication is not always possible, and even when it is possible it may not always be judged necessary. Michael Polanyi provides an example of this last point:

> A series of simple experiments were published in June 1947 in the *Proceedings of the Royal Society* by Lord Rayleigh – a distinguished Fellow of the Society – purporting to show that hydrogen atoms striking a metal wire transmit to it energies up to a hundred electron volts. This, if true, would have been far more revolutionary than the discovery of atomic fission by Otto Hahn. Yet, when I asked physicists what they thought about it, they only shrugged their shoulders. They could not find fault with the experiment yet not one believed in its results, nor thought it worth while to repeat it. They just ignored it. (. . .) It appeared that the physicists missed nothing by disregarding these findings. (Polanyi, 1968: 4–5)

I would not want to deny that the assessment of claims in the natural sciences is often more conclusive than it is in the social sciences; and that replication makes some contribution to this. However, even in the natural sciences there is an ineradicable element of judgement and uncertainty involved in the process of assessing the products of research. Natural scientists do not operate on the basis of the mechanical formula: if replication reproduces the findings accept them, if it does not then reject them. Rather, they *interpret* the product and process of the research in terms of the plausibility of the findings and the effects of likely sources of error, and then make a judgement about validity on this basis. Replication may be an important aid for them in making this judgement, but it cannot replace the judgement; and sometimes judgement is (or has to be) made without the aid of replication.

So, the argument that ethnographic studies are not scientific because they cannot easily be replicated is based on a false conception of the role of replication in natural science. Our inability to replicate ethnographic findings does not undermine assessments of their validity, though it may make the task more difficult.

Let me turn now to questioning of the criterion of validity from the other direction: on the grounds that the very idea that ethnographic accounts represent an independent social reality is doubtful. There are at least two arguments used to support such doubts.

One is that the use of the term 'truth' implies the possession of knowledge that is absolutely certain (that is proven beyond all possible doubt), yet knowledge can never be certain in this sense. These critics point out that in deciding on the validity or otherwise of some claim we always rely on assumptions whose own validity we must presuppose. And if we seek to test any of those presuppositions, we shall be forced to rely on further assumptions. For instance, even in simple measurements of physical objects with a ruler, we make assumptions about the properties of rigid bodies (that is, of both ruler and object); such as that small changes in temperature will not have any significant effect on our measurements. And testing those assumptions would involve (among other things) measuring heat, which itself involves assumptions about the operation of thermometers, and so on.

In my view the second half of this argument is sound; but the first (that use of the concept of truth implies knowledge that is certain beyond all possible doubt) is not. To claim that something is true is not incompatible with a recognition that our judgement about it may be wrong. I believe that we can *never* be absolutely certain about the truth of anything, not even in the natural sciences or in our personal lives. On the other hand, there are many things about whose truth we are very confident and about which we have every right to be confident. What I am arguing here is that we can have good reasons for believing that something is true or false without ever being absolutely certain about the validity of the claim. We rely on a whole host of assumptions about the world in our everyday lives, and while many of them are probably approximately true, we can never be absolutely sure of the truth of any of them. Yet, this ever-present uncertainty does not undermine our use of the concept of truth.

A second source of problems with 'truth' arises from beliefs about the nature of human social life. There are those who hold that in the case of social phenomena there is no single reality to which ethnographic claims may correspond. It is argued that it is characteristic of human beings that they create multiple social worlds or realities, that all perception and cognition involves the *construction* of phenomena rather than their mere discovery. From this point of view, there are multiple social realities or worlds, not just a single one; and it may be concluded that contradictory views of 'the same' phenomena by different cultural groups are equally 'true' in their own terms. This argument is developed in a sophisticated form by Peter Winch in his criticisms of Evans-Pritchard's famous account of witchcraft among the Azande of central Africa. Winch notes that while seeking to understand Zande beliefs and practices, Evans-Pritchard nonetheless treats them as false and ineffective because of what he 'knows' about reality on the basis of Western science. Winch argues, however, that this 'knowledge' is founded on a conception of reality that is presupposed by science rather than being independent of it, just as the Zande conception of reality is presupposed by *their* beliefs and practices. In other words, there is no independent basis on which we can judge between these two conceptions. In these terms magic is as real for the Azande as the reality depicted by science (or at least some of it!) is for us; there is no ground for claiming that the latter is 'more real' (Winch, 1964).[6]

Of course, if we apply this argument to social research itself, we might see the latter as creating its own world (or, given the dissensus among social scientists, its own worlds). As we saw earlier, an example of such anti-realism is to be found among those who have given attention to the character of ethnographic texts. Some have claimed that these texts do not represent an independent reality, but *create* the social worlds they purport to describe through textual strategies of various kinds. And these strategies are a reflection of Western culture. Effectively, the argument here is not just that we can never be sure of the truth or falsity of our claims about reality but that we have no grounds for believing that there is an independent reality, since all the knowledge we can ever have is formed by our culture; and that culture is only one of many.

While this argument makes an important point about the limits and difficulties placed on understanding by cultural diversity, the conclusion that there is no reality independent of the researcher for her or him to document does not follow from it. All social phenomena are human products and are therefore (in some senses) not independent of humanity as a whole. But much social life *is* independent of any particular researcher or group of researchers. Furthermore, we are able to learn other cultures to one degree or another, and thereby to understand human behaviour that is framed in terms of them. That implies some commonalities among cultures on which knowledge may be built. It is also worth pointing out that to claim that there are other cultures, or even that one's own views represent a culture, itself implies the claim that there is an independent world in which those cultures are to be found. Therefore, anti-realism or relativism of this kind is self-contradictory.

These two anti-realist arguments about truth count against 'naive realism': the idea that there is a single world independent of us about which we have direct (and therefore certain) knowledge. And to the extent that ethnography is wedded to such a view, as it often seems to be under the influence of naturalism, these arguments are sound criticisms of it. However, in taking account of these arguments, we do not need to abandon the concept of truth as correspondence to an independent reality. We can retain this concept of truth by adopting a more subtle realism. I have already introduced the key elements of this point of view, but they can be summarised as follows:

(a) No knowledge is certain, but knowledge claims can be judged reasonably accurately in terms of their likely truth.
(b) There are phenomena independent of us as researchers or readers of which we can have knowledge (but only in the sense defined above).

In my view, then, there is no reason to abandon the concept of truth or validity as a criterion for assessing research findings, even though naive interpretations of it must be rejected.

Of course, even if we accept that validity is a feasible and legitimate criterion in terms of which to assess ethnographic research, the question remains: On what basis can assessment be carried out, given that replication is so difficult and that there is no foundation of knowledge by means of which an ethnographer can validate her or his account? The only basis left, it seems to me, is our judgements of the likelihood of error. From this point of view, there are three steps in assessing the validity of ethnographic claims:

1. The first question that we must ask about a claim is whether it seems plausible; that is, whether we judge it as very likely to be true given our existing knowledge. In the case of some claims, they will be so plausible that we can reasonably accept them at face value, without needing to know anything about how the writer came to formulate them or what evidence there is to support them. The first test, then, is plausibility.
2. A second question we may need to ask is whether it seems likely that the ethnographer's judgement of matters relating to the claim would be accurate given the nature of the phenomena concerned, the circumstances of the research, the characteristics of the researcher, etc. I shall call this 'credibility'. As with plausibility, there are claims whose credibility is such that we can reasonably accept them without further ado.
3. Where we conclude that a claim is neither sufficiently plausible

nor sufficiently credible, we will require evidence to be convinced of its validity. However, when we examine the evidence we shall have to employ much the same means to assess its validity as we applied to the claim itself: we shall judge *its* plausibility and credibility. And, of course, we may require further evidence to support that evidence, which we shall again judge in terms of plausibility and credibility.

In many respects, this seems to me to be the sort of basis on which we judge claims, our own and those of others, in everyday life. This is not done on a purely individual basis of course. As co-participants in various communal activities we compare our judgements with those of others; and where there are disagreements and agreement must be reached this may be produced in a variety of ways, including debate, but also by means of negotiation, delegation, majority decision, or even the exercise of coercion.

Needless to say, plausibility and credibility form a relatively weak basis for judging claims, compared to the idea that we can assess claims directly according to their correspondence with reality or by relying on some body of knowledge whose validity is certain. This approach provides no guarantee that our judgements will be correct, nor any way of knowing for certain whether they are correct. Nor will judgements necessarily be consensual, since there may be different views about what is plausible and credible. And the effect of treating the basis on which validity is assessed in science as similar to its assessment in everyday life is to de-emphasise the difference between the two; whereas it has often been claimed that science has distinctive and superior access to the truth.

We must accept the weakness of this basis, I think, but recognise that it is the only one we have, and that it does not exclude the possibility of cumulative knowledge. Furthermore, I am not suggesting that there should be no differences between everyday assessments of validity and those carried out in the natural and social sciences. The key difference, in my view, is that researchers specialise in inquiry, whereas in everyday life inquiry is a minor and subordinate element of other activities. And the other side of this is that the publication of research findings involves a claim to authority; and such publications are often accorded more authority than the judgements of non-researchers. We must ask, therefore, on what basis this authority can be founded. The justification seems to me to lie in a form of social organisation that subjects claims to a more severe level of routine validity checking than is common in most other spheres of life and involves sustained attempts to resolve disagreements by debate and further inquiry, rather than by other means. From this point of view, the scientific community should have three key features:

1. All findings are subjected to communal assessment in which there

is an effort to resolve disagreements by seeking common grounds of agreement and trying to work back to a resolution of the dispute relying only on what is accepted as valid by all disputants. This rules out the dismissal of arguments on the basis of the personal and social characteristics of the person advancing them.

2. Scientists are willing to change their views if such arguments from common ground suggest those views to be false; and they assume (and behave as if) fellow scientists have the same attitude.

3. The scientific community is open to participation by anyone able and willing to operate on the basis of the first two rules.

A scientific community operating according to these rules maximises the chances of discovering error in assumptions about what is plausible and credible. It also maximises the possibility of rational consensus. In these ways it encourages the cumulative development of knowledge; and it is for this reason that scientific knowledge is more likely to be true than are commonsense views about the same issues. This is not to say that in any particular instance current scientific knowledge will be correct and commonsense wrong; simply that scientific knowledge is likely to be closer to the truth on the average. Furthermore, it should be noted that this advantage is bought at some cost in terms of the time taken to resolve inquiries in this way.

Even natural science does not conform perfectly to this ideal of communal organisation; though it probably approximates it more closely than does social science.[7] In the natural sciences obstacles to the operation of the three rules are likely to come mainly from individuals' personal commitment to particular theories and facts on the basis of their career interests.[8] While other interests, such as religious and political commitments, play a role in some areas of natural science (such as evolution and nuclear power), in general they have little influence. In the social sciences, on the other hand, such commitments have a much more wide-ranging influence because the topics investigated usually have much more direct social significance. Such commitments have the effect of reducing the likelihood that views will be changed on the basis of counter-argument, and that others will be seen as prepared to change their views. Nevertheless, it seems to me that, to the extent that social scientists have an obligation to maximise the chances that their findings are valid, the aim should be to approximate the process of assessment that this model implies. What this means is that in judging claims we must rely not just on our own assumptions about their plausibility and credibility, but also on what we take as likely to be the consensus among other members of the research community. Anything that we do not find plausible or credible, or that we believe a substantial number of others will not find plausible or credible, requires support from evidence that *is* so regarded. And, just as researchers must write with the anticipated assumptions of their audience in mind, providing evidence sufficient to convince that audience, so we as readers must judge claims not only in relation to our own assumptions but also in relation to those that we expect to be accepted as beyond reasonable doubt by other members of the research community.

Truth or validity is the first criterion, then, in terms of which I believe that ethnographic accounts should be judged; and in the next chapter I will look at how this should be done in more detail. Before doing that, though, we must look at the second criterion, what I have called 'relevance'.

RELEVANCE

In my view, to be of value research findings must not only be valid but also be relevant to issues of public concern. This second criterion is curiously neglected in most treatments of social research methodology. It is rarely mentioned explicitly in discussions of criteria, whether those appealing to the quantitative tradition or those offering distinctive ethnographic criteria. One reason for this may be the influence on ethnographic thinking of what I have called naturalism and the naive realism associated with it. As I noted in Chapter 2, these ideas may lead us to believe that descriptions reproduce the phenomena to which they refer, thereby encouraging neglect of the multiple descriptions possible of any phenomenon. But it is important to recognise that reality is infinite in scope, and that any part of it can be described in a large number of ways.[9] And, given this, ethnographers cannot take their task as being simply to describe the social world. They, and we as readers, must decide which facts are important and are therefore worth describing, and which are not.

So, our interest in facts (in everyday life as much as in social research) is selective. All descriptions are for some purpose, and the nature of the purpose will crucially shape the character of the description. If, say, we are describing a meeting, it will make a considerable difference whether our interest is in the political positions that are represented, the differential participation of men and women, variation in the form of public debate between this setting and similar situations in other cultures, or something else. The descriptions produced on the basis of these various interests may overlap, but equally they may be so different as to be not recognisably referring to the same meeting (though if we believe that they are all true they should not contradict one another). And there are any number of points of view from which we can describe a social phenomenon. So, too, with explanations. These will not only be concerned with accounting for some aspects of a phenomenon rather than others, but will also involve the selection of explanatory factors in terms of the purpose which the explanation is to serve.

It is also of significance in this context that ethnographic accounts are communications addressed to an audience. When we communicate with people they assume that we are telling them something that is likely to be of significance to them. If it turns out that we merely communicate facts, any facts, we shall soon find that we have few listeners.[10] In the case of most social research the aim is to communicate with a relatively large audience (otherwise what would be the point of publication?); and it follows that what is communicated should be relevant in some way to such an audience. The obvious questions that follow from this are: Who are the appropriate audience(s)? and What sort of relevance should social research have for them?

As we saw in Chapter 1, one of the main criticisms of ethnography in recent times has come from those urging a closer relationship with practice. This amounts to the argument that practitioners (members of various occupations, interest groups, political parties, etc.) should be the audience for research and that it should serve their purposes directly. This argument can be found among both those committed to the natural science paradigm and those who reject it.

Among the former are advocates of what is often called the 'engineering' or 'applied science' model. Here particular pieces of research are to be judged in terms of whether (and how well) they resolve some problem faced by a group of practitioners. This view is typically associated with the idea that practical problems are generally the result of inadequate knowledge and can be resolved by the application of scientific method, with science perhaps eventually replacing ordinary practical knowledge.

To date, this view has had relatively little impact on ethnography; though with the growing use of qualitative methods in applied research – often contracted by Government departments that are under increasing pressure for accountability – greater influence is likely in the future. Perhaps more significantly, it is also the view that some practitioners take of the function of research, and is one of the bases on which research is sometimes judged by them to be irrelevant to their needs.

Somewhat more influential among ethnographers has been what I referred to in Chapter 1 as the emancipatory model. The main source here is Marxism. For Marx, as the famous quote has it, the point was not to understand the world but to change it (Marx, 1845). Thus, there is always pressure within Marxist scholarship for it to demonstrate its relevance to political practice; and some Marxists have conceptualised this link with practice in strong and direct terms. For example, Georg Lukacs believed that the work of Marxist intellectuals should be integral to the operation of the Communist Party, conceived as the bearer of proletarian consciousness. He viewed this consciousness as an aspect of socio-historical process in which the Party comes to understand the world through transforming it. There is little scope for any independent role for intellectuals here.[11]

An approach which allows somewhat more leeway, but retains the strong link with practice, is the critical theory developed by the Frankfurt School, especially Jurgen Habermas. Critical theories are designed to produce emancipation of oppressed groups through enlightenment; that is, by enabling members of such groups to recognise their true interests. It is claimed that ideology prevents oppressed groups from understanding their situation and interests, and is therefore a major factor in sustaining their oppression. A central feature of the work of critical theorists is therefore ideology-critique. Research inspired by critical theory differs from conventional ethnography in at least two respects. First, the aim is not primarily to describe (or even to explain) the culture of the people studied but to identify the effects of ideology on that culture. Second, the success or otherwise of a 'critical theory' in bringing about enlightenment and emancipation is a crucial, perhaps *the* crucial, aspect of any assessment of its validity. Here Habermas uses an analogy with psychoanalysis. The validity of psychoanalytic interpretations is partly judged by whether they are recognised as true by the patient and whether that recognition eliminates the symptoms; in other words they are judged by the success or otherwise of the therapeutic process, viewed as a self-reflective movement towards personal autonomy. In short, the critical theory sets out to explain the nature of a social order in such a way that it serves as a catalyst for the transformation of that order.[12]

Similar ideas are to be found in some recent feminist writing about methodology. Many feminists define the goal of their research as the emancipation of women, rather than as the production of valid knowledge in itself.[13] Often combined with this is the claim that the truth can only be discovered in and through the struggle against women's oppression. And, as in the case of Habermas, this argument is sometimes taken one step further, suggesting that truth is to be judged in terms of contribution to the goal of emancipation:

(. . .) the 'truth' of a theory is not dependent on the application of certain methodological principles and rules, but on its potential to orient the processes of praxis towards progressive emancipation and humanization. (Mies, 1983: 124)

Here validity as a criterion is itself redefined in terms of a strong interpretation of relevance.

In my view, neither of these views advocating a very close relationship between research and practice is convincing. The applied science model adopts too narrow a conception of the contribution that research can make to practice, allowing it to be constrained by practitioners' perspectives. Much of the value of research, it seems to me, is that it addresses issues that are not of immediate concern to any particular set of practitioners, but which are nevertheless important. The most pressing problems are not always the most significant, nor can we assume that practitioners have a solid understanding of their problems or of their situations. We need not accept the rather monolithic conception of ideology adopted by critical theorists to recognise that people's understandings of their world (and I am including researchers in this) are subject to biases and distortions of various kinds. We must not, therefore, treat practitioners' perspectives as automatically beyond reasonable doubt. Researchers must be free to question practitioner assumptions where this seems necessary.

By contrast, the emancipatory model suffers from too narrow a conception of the appropriate audience for research. It seems to be restricted to members of the group to be emancipated. This may be because, as in the case of most versions of feminism, the emancipation of this group has been adopted as the primary goal, and it is believed that emancipation must come from 'below' not 'above'. Presumably, from this point of view, other sorts of research, directed towards different goals and audiences, are legitimate (if less important). However, there is a version of the emancipatory model, most clearly exemplified in Marxism, in which the target oppressed group is effectively the only legitimate audience since only it has the capacity to emancipate all humanity. This is the historic mission assigned to the proletariat by Marx and Lukacs (though not by Habermas). But we must ask: What reason is there to believe that the proletariat or any other group has such a historic mission? And there seems to me to be no good reason to believe it (Hammersley, 1990f).

It is perhaps also worth noting that what is narrowly constrained in the emancipatory model is not just the audience but also the range of topics that are judged to be important. Only those directly related to the task of emancipation (however conceived) are relevant. This is a problem that extends beyond this model. The discipline of sociology has built into it a set of assumptions about what are important research topics. Sociology began in the nineteenth century with an interest in the effects of socio-economic change on society, viewed from the point of view of the twin values of equality and social order; and the issues that arose in that context (inequality, class conflict, urbanisation, bureaucratisation, democratisation, the apparent loss of community, etc.) remain at its centre. Other topics have been added; for example, those arising from the discipline's role in the education of new professional groups – social workers, teachers, medical professionals, etc. The result is a rather hotchpotch pattern of interests in terms of which topics are judged to be important and unimportant. This is something that has been highlighted by feminist critiques, which have pointed to the male-oriented character of many of the central issues dealt with by social research, and the neglect and low status given to topics that are often of greater importance to women: family life, child-bearing, the care of young children, the lives of working women, etc. This underlines the point that we must take care not to adopt an overly restrictive conception of what are relevant topics for research on the basis of conventional views that do not stand up to close scrutiny.

Perhaps even more important than these points, however, is that both the applied science and emancipatory models misconceive the nature of practice, and effectively overestimate the contribution that research can make to it. Commonly associated with the applied science model, as the name implies, is the idea that practice can take the form of the mere application of scientific knowledge. What is involved here, it is assumed, is the implementation of rules or prescriptions.[14] However, this is not a plausible conception of the nature of practice, as a variety of recent writers have argued (Schwab, 1978; Lindblom and Cohen, 1979; Schon, 1987; Larmore, 1987; Carr, 1987). To varying degrees these writers draw on a conception of the nature of practice that goes back at least to Aristotle (Lobkowicz, 1967). Aristotle drew a sharp distinction between, on the one hand, theoretical science, involving the contemplation of eternal truths and, on the other, the more uncertain knowledge on which practical activities, like politics, are based and which derives from experience. Building on these views, practice may be seen to involve making decisions in the light of multiple, schematic (and possibly conflicting) values that have to be interpreted in relation to concrete and changing situations about which we have limited information. It is *not* the pursuit of some fixed end state, but the preservation or improvement of a situation in the light of a set of values whose validity one accepts for the moment (while recognising that they may need to be revised subsequently). Furthermore, in the course of such action we must take account of the likely consequences for other values and interests of any strategies and tactics employed. What I am emphasising here is the inevitably contextual character of practice; not just of judgement about what would be effective means, but even of assessments of appropriate and reasonable goals.

If this view of practice is correct, while Aristotle may have been wrong to suggest that theory has no implications for practice, it is clear (I think) that the knowledge produced by research cannot provide a basis for deducing the most appropriate practical courses of action in a particular situation. The potential role of research is much more limited than this.

While Habermas criticises the view of practice implied by the applied science model (Habermas, 1973), in effect critical theory adopts a similarly ambitious conception of the relationship between theory and practice. Here the goal of practice is conceived as being to bring reality into line with theory. This is a view that derives from Marx and Hegel, both of whom regarded practice as taking place within a historical process conceived as leading (potentially at least) to the self-realisation of humanity, to an era of human freedom in which people's lives would exemplify the ideals that previously had been striven for but had been unachievable. In these terms, the view of practice I sketched above is treated as an accurate portrayal of life before emancipation, but not of human life as it ought to be *and as it will be*. However, in my judgement this perspective is utopian. There are no good reasons for supposing that the character of practice will be completely transformed in the manner claimed, and even less that this will be brought about by practice based on critical theory.

Besides misconstruing the character of practice, these advocates of a close relationship between research and practice also overestimate the capacity of research to produce information that is needed by practitioners. Both seem to assume that whatever knowledge is required can be produced, and in a relatively straightforward way. While I would not want to declare *any* knowledge unobtainable in principle, I think it is clear that sometimes the knowledge that we would like is not easily accessible. After all, we have long wished to know more about cancer so as to prevent or cure it, and very considerable resources have been expended in pursuit of that knowledge. But while we now know a lot more than we did, we still lack some of the knowledge that we need. What this highlights is that producing the knowledge which is needed may take a long time and require more resources than are available. Furthermore, and this is a very important point, it may well involve a complex division of labour among researchers; the result of which will be that many of the studies carried out will have only indirect relevance to the original problem. This recognition of the importance of a division of labour among researchers also implies that fellow researchers will often be the primary audience for research reports, even though the eventual outcome of the research process should be relevant for practitioners.

I have argued, then, that to be of value research findings must have public relevance, but that this must not be interpreted as implying that every research project, and even less every research report, must make a direct contribution of knowledge required by some narrowly defined group of practitioners. Rather, researchers must be allowed, first, to address issues which are not of immediate concern to practitioners but which there are reasonable grounds for believing are of relevance to their practice; second, to address a wide variety of practitioner audiences; and, third, to operate a division of labour so that other researchers will often serve as the primary audience for many research reports. Furthermore, the limitations on the capacity of research to contribute to practice must be recognised: limitations that arise from the nature of both practice and research.

There is another important issue that I have not addressed so far. We may all agree that research should be relevant to practice (even if differing about the details), but the question arises: What sort of arguments can be used to decide about relevance? After all, is this not an issue that involves value judgements in which people may simply disagree because they have different values?

As we saw in Chapter 1, a significant feature of social research in the twentieth century has been the drive to make it scientific. And despite the variety of intepretations of this ideal, a common element has been the view that science deals only with factual issues and that value issues lie outside its scope, with the implication often being drawn that they are therefore outside the range of rational deliberation. The basis for this restriction is the belief that while factual issues are open to rigorous investigation on the basis of evidence leading to consensus, the same is not true of value issues. However, as we saw, developments in the philosophy of science over this century have undercut the idea that factual issues are so easily resolvable. And our discussion of validity in the previous section reinforces this. Some have concluded from the difficulties involved in establishing the validity of factual claims that cognitive relativism should be added to the value relativism that has previously been taken to be essential to science; so that we must simply accept that there are multiple, contradictory, but equally valid, views of the world. In discussing the criterion of validity I tried to show why I think that this is neither necessary nor advisable. Here I want to suggest that much the same sort of solution can be applied to the problem of value disputes as was suggested for factual disputes. In both cases, the key to the pursuit of truth, though in neither case offering a guarantee, is to rely on judgements of plausibility and credibility; and, in the face of disagreement, to search for common ground that is accepted by both sides, working back from there to some conclusion about the disputed issue by drawing only on assumptions that are accepted as valid by both sides. This is a controversial, and by no means easy, approach, but it is the one I shall adopt in illustrating the application of the criterion of relevance in Chapter 5.

CONCLUSION

In this chapter I have looked at the issue of the criteria in terms of which ethnographic studies should be assessed. I argued that neither those approaches that sought to apply the criteria used in quantitative research, nor those advocating distinctive ethnographic criteria, are satisfactory as they stand, though both capture important aspects of the process of assessment. I put forward two criteria for the assessment of any social research: validity and relevance. I tried to show that the arguments that have been used to question the appropriateness of applying the criterion of validity to ethnography are not convincing, and that it is a reasonable standard of assessment. I also outlined something of the process by means of which validity could be assessed. In discussing the criterion of relevance, I sought to establish its importance, to clarify how it should be interpreted, and to outline the basis on which judgements about relevance could be justified. In the following chapters I shall look in more detail at the use of these two criteria in the assessment of ethnographic research.

NOTES

1. In the terms I used in the previous chapter, every causal claim about events within an experiment is an explanation, and therefore relies on at least one theoretical assumption.
2. The emphasis on theory may be an aspect of the concern with the scientificity of ethnography and its distinctiveness from common-sense. One of the problems with naturalistic accounts for ethnographers is that they may appear to be nothing more than reproductions of common knowledge and therefore of little value.
3. The distinction between substantive and formal theory comes from Glaser and Strauss (1967). Substantive theory deals with particular empirical areas like patient care, race relations, delinquency, etc. Formal theory is concerned with more abstract areas of sociological inquiry such as stigma, deviant behaviour, authority and power, etc.
4. This is analogous to some quantitative methodologists' attempts to define validity and reliability in terms of the results of the measurement process, rather than in terms of a relationship between measurements and what they were intended to measure. (The classic case of this is, of course, the definition of intelligence as: what intelligence tests measure.) In this chapter I am concerned with criteria as standards rather than with the means by which we assess studies in terms of those standards. I shall address the latter issue in Chapter 4.
5. This is another instance of the selectivity of description, and of the uncertainty surrounding what should and should not be treated as relevant to a particular description.
6. For a development of this sort of argument into a 'critique of scientific reason', see Feyerabend (1975 and 1978) and Siegel (1989).
7. Scholarship in some other areas, such as some parts of the humanities, may also approximate this model quite closely.
8. Scientific research in commercial organisations and the increasing commercialisation of research in higher education institutions involve additional threats, however. For instance, their encouragement of increased secrecy (because sales depend on confidence in products that could be undermined by public debate)

threatens the very basis of the scientific community as I have defined it.

9. This point and its implications are explored at length by Rickert. For an excellent summary, see Oakes (1988).

10. Of course, we do not merely communicate facts in everyday life; there are other forms of discourse, like questions, requests, commands, promises, etc. But I am assuming that this is the primary form of discourse in social research. On the assumption of relevance in conversation, see Sperber and Wilson (1986).

11. See Lichtheim (1970), Kolakowski (1978), and/or Jay (1984).

12. An example of an ethnographic study strongly influenced by the emancipatory model is Willis (1977).

13. See, for example, Mies (1983) and Harding (1987).

14. What I have referred to here as the 'applied science' model is an extreme version of what is sometimes called the 'engineering model, see Janowitz 1971 and Bulmer 1982a: Ch.2.

Making an assessment: validity

In discussing the criterion of validity in the previous chapter, I advocated a position which I called 'subtle realism'. While retaining the idea that true knowledge corresponds in relevant respects to the phenomena that we seek to represent, this view recognises that we can never be absolutely certain about the validity of any knowledge claim; but it suggests that we can still make reasonable judgements about the likely validity of such claims. I also outlined the implications of this position for assessing the validity of ethnographic findings: that it involves assessing their plausibility and credibility, and (where necessary) that of any evidence provided. Here I want to discuss this process of assessment in more detail, looking first at the examination of major claims and the evidence supporting them, and then at the assessment of conclusions about the research focus drawn on the basis of those claims.

ASSESSING MAJOR CLAIMS AND EVIDENCE

In making an assessment of an ethnographic study we must begin by taking each of its major claims and asking how plausible that claim is on the basis of our existing knowledge. Let us say we are faced with the following two claims, from Strong's study of paediatric consultations in Britain and the United States:

1. There was variation in whether both parents attended the consultation, and where only one attended it was usually the mother.
2. Where the father alone accompanied the child he was treated as a loving but incompetent substitute for the mother.

The first of these two claims seems to me to be very plausible, on the basis of what I (and I assume we all) know about British and US society, including experience of doctors' waiting rooms. I do not need any evidence or even any information about how the researcher came to this conclusion in order to accept its validity. And I suspect that others would not need evidence to be convinced either. In the case of the second claim, however, I am not inclined simply to accept it. It is not that I find it implausible, but rather that it is not *so* plausible that it can be accepted at face value.

Some of the major claims in ethnographic studies may be so plausible that they need no support.[1] Many, however, will not be. Faced with a claim that is not sufficiently plausible to be accepted, the second step is to assess its credibility (as I defined this term in Chapter 3). Here the task is to decide whether the claim is of such a kind that an ethnographer, given what is known of the circumstances of the research, could have made a judgement about the validity of this claim with a reasonably low chance of error. Here, of course, we must use what knowledge we have, or what we can reasonably assume, about how the research was carried out. For instance, we must look at whether the research involved the ethnographer's own observations or reliance on the accounts of informants, or both; what role the ethnographer adopted in the field; etc. What must be estimated here are *both* the likelihood of error given the nature of the phenomenon *and* the chances of error because of the character of the ethnographer's or informant's access to it and/or because of bias on their part.[2]

As an illustration of such judgements about credibility, let us consider the research of Ray Rist into the effects of teachers' expectations on pupils' school performance (Rist, 1970). In the course of his study, Rist makes claims about which pupils were put into which classroom groups by the kindergarten teacher he studied. In my view we can conclude that his judgement of this distribution is rather unlikely to be wrong, given that it involves a relatively simple matter of observation, that he observed the class regularly over a relatively long period, and that on this issue he seems unlikely to have been affected by bias. However, Rist also makes the claim that the three groups of children received differential treatment by the teacher. In my view we should not accept this simply on the basis of his presence as observer in the situation. This is because multiple and uncertain judgements are involved, in the form of observations about amounts and types of attention given to pupils by the teacher over a lengthy period of time. Thus, while we might reasonably accept Rist's first claim as credible on the basis of what we know about his research, I do not believe that we should accept his second claim on the same basis.

If we find a claim very plausible or highly credible, then we should be prepared to accept it without evidence. However, if we judge a claim to be neither sufficiently plausible nor credible, then we must look to see whether the author has provided any evidence to support it. If not, then our conclusion should be that judgement must be suspended. If evidence *is* provided we must assess the validity of that evidence. And where that evidence is itself supported by further evidence, we may need to assess the latter too. As we saw in Chapter 2, claims can be of several types, and different sorts of evidence are appropriate to each. Below, I shall look at each type of claim and the evidence required to support it.

DEFINITIONS

Definitions are not empirical claims about the world but statements about how the author is going to use a term, about what meaning is to be associated with it. As such, they are not likely to form part of the main claims of ethnographic studies. However, they may be an important element of the evidence required for such claims. And while they are not open to assessment in the same manner as factual claims, this does not mean that they are open to no assessment at all.

One obvious assessment we can make of a definition is whether it has sufficient clarity for the purposes being pursued. Where there is a standard usage of a term that is clear enough for the purposes at hand, no definition is required. However many social scientific concepts are ambiguous or uncertain in meaning, and yet are often used without definition. A notorious example is 'social class', which can have very different definitions, based on discrepant theoretical assumptions (for example those of Marx and Weber); though usage often relies on vague and less coherent assumptions. And many other concepts raise similar problems.

One that is quite frequently employed in ethnographic research today is 'subculture'. This term seems to have been introduced into US sociology in the late 1940s to refer to:

a sub-division of national culture, composed of a combination of factorable social situations such as class status, ethnic background, regional and rural or urban residence, religious affiliation, but *forming in their combination a functioning unity which has an integrated impact on the participating individual.* (Gordon, 1947: 40)

In the 1960s and 1970s 'subculture' became widely used in claiming that different social classes had distinctive life styles, beliefs and values and in the explanation of crime and delinquency. Both these applications involved a shift from Gordon's definition. The first made one factor (social class) central, rather than interpreting the subculture as a product of the integrated effects of multiple factors. Usage of the term in the study of delinquency and crime diverged from its original definition in identifying delinquent subcultures primarily in terms of a commitment to one or another kind of deviant or criminal act. Another variation in interpretation is that whereas Gordon identified subcultures in terms of an observer's judgement about 'functioning unity', in much subsequent usage of the term a key element is participants' recognition of belonging to a distinctive group. Indeed, 'subculture' is sometimes used effectively as a technical synonym for 'group'.[3] Such a usage raises problems like: do different groups with similar life-styles belong to the same subculture or are they merely similar subcultures? And if the former, how similar must they be to belong to the same subculture? Equally, we might ask how much change in beliefs, attitudes and behaviour is allowed before we must conclude that one subculture has died and another been born (or that a group has changed from one subculture to another)? Also, can a single person be a member of more than one subculture at the same time, or is membership of any subculture all-encompassing? And, as if this were not enough, it is worth pointing out that Gordon's original definition is by no means unproblematic. He describes subcultures as subdivisions of national cultures; but the term culture is itself ambiguous, sometimes being almost identical in meaning to 'society' (which seems to be the way Gordon uses the term), sometimes referring to beliefs and values rather than to actions and structures (and therefore being part of, or related to, rather than isomorphic with societies). This ambiguity is inherited by 'subculture'. While the term 'subculture' is widely used, these conceptual issues are rarely addressed, and sometimes vagueness and uncertainty cause problems.[4] Nor are 'social class' and 'subculture' unusual in this respect. What has been said about them is true of other concepts that are routinely used in ethnographic studies.

Faced with uncertainty about the meaning of key concepts (whether or not definitions are provided) we must give attention to two aspects of that meaning; intension (the concept's relationship to other concepts) and extension (its relationship to instances).

To clarify intension, we must identify other elements of the network to which the concept belongs. Concepts get some of their meaning by forming part of a set of distinctions that is hierarchically organised. I can illustrate this by looking again at Woods' contrast between teaching and survival strategies on the part of secondary school teachers (see Chapter 2; Woods, 1979a: ch.7). We can note that despite their differences, these are sub-types of a higher level category: teacher strategies. This opens up the question of what other types of classroom action teachers engage in besides strategies. Similarly, at the other end of this conceptual network, Woods himself identifies a variety of different sorts of survival strategies. Putting these two points together, we can see how the distinction between teaching and survival strategies forms part of a larger conceptual structure which can be represented diagrammatically by Figure 1.

By mapping out conceptual networks of this kind we may be able to see weaknesses in the formulation of key terms. In the case of Woods' study, it seems to me that the distinction between strategies and other forms of classroom action on the part of teachers stands out as requiring clarification. This would specify the meaning of 'survival strategy'.

Figure 1 *Woods' model of teachers' strategies*

The second aspect of meaning, extension, concerns what would and would not count as instances of each category. Sometimes the problem of identifying instances may be quite difficult. Staying with the example from Woods, he argues that survival strategies

(. . .) expand into teaching and around it, like some parasitic plant, and eventually in some cases the host might be completely killed off. However, like parasites, if they kill off the host, they are a failure and they must die too, for they stand starkly revealed for what they are. The best strategies are those that allow a modicum of education to seep through. Alternatively, they will appear as teaching, their survival value having a higher premium than their educational value. (Woods, 1979a: 146–7)

While the definition of survival is reasonably clear in its intension, its extension is problematic: given that the concern with survival may masquerade as teaching, and that survival strategies may have educational value, how are we to distinguish instances of the two? This is not a problem that Woods addresses, but in my judgement it is of considerable importance if we are to assess the validity of his claims.[5]

Another basis on which we may criticise definitions is that they fail to make distinctions that we believe are important, given the goal of the research. An example arises in Jean Anyon's report of a study of teacher–pupil relations in five elementary schools in the United States that catered for pupils from catchment areas differing sharply in social-class composition. In presenting her findings she provides the following discussion:

A dominant theme that emerged in these two schools was student *resistance*. Although some amount of resistance appeared in every school in this study, in the working-class schools it was a dominant characteristic of student–teacher interaction. In the fifth grades there was both active and passive resistance to teachers' attempts to impose the curriculum. Active sabotage sometimes took place: someone put a bug in one student's desk; boys fell out of their chairs; they misplaced books; or forgot them; they engaged in minor theft from each other; sometimes they rudely interrupted the teacher. When I asked the children during interviews why they did these things they said, 'To get the teacher mad'; 'Because he don't teach us nothin''; 'They give us too many punishments'. When I asked them what the teachers *should* do, they said, 'Teach us some more'; 'Take us alone and help us'; 'Help us learn'.

The children also engaged in a good deal of resistance that was more passive. They often resisted by withholding their enthusiasm or attention on occasions when the teacher attempted to do something special. (. . .) Passive resistance can also be seen on some occasions when the children do not respond to the teacher's questions. For example, they sit just staring at the board or the teacher while the teacher tries to get them to say the answer, any answer. On one such occasion, the teacher shouted sarcastically across the room to me, 'Just *look* at the motivation on their faces'. On occasions when teachers finally explode with impatience because nobody 'knows' the answer, one can see fleeting smiles flicker across some of the students' faces: they are pleased to see the teacher get angry, upset. (Anyon, 1981: 11–12)

It has been argued, with some justification I think, that the concept of resistance used by Anyon is insufficiently discriminating. As Hargreaves comments:

the mistake Anyon makes is to assume that acts of overt social protest are of the same nature as more minor transgressions, pranks and absences of enthusiasm (. . .) Almost all pupil actions that fall short of absolute and willing compliance to teachers' demands are counted as resistance by her. (Hargreaves, 1984: 31–2).

He contrasts this usage with the more restricted one found among other writers on pupils' orientation to school. They often distinguish a wide range of pupil adaptations, and recognise that not all of pupils' actions in the classroom are oriented primarily towards the teacher (Furlong, 1976; Woods, 1979a; Hammersley and Turner, 1980).

Definitions may be an important part of ethnographic accounts, then; and even where they are absent they may need to be reconstructed (as far as is possible). While they cannot be judged in empirical terms, we can assess their clarity and whether they make what seem to be necessary distinctions, given the purposes of the research.

DESCRIPTIONS

Descriptions are accounts of the features of some set of phenomena (one or more) that exists (or has existed) in a particular place and time. The phenomena studied may vary in number and size (geographically and/or temporally). For example, at one extreme we may study the first five seconds of a few telephone calls (Schegloff, 1968); at the other, we may investigate the development over time of factory work relations in several contemporary societies (Burawoy, 1985). Most ethnographic research deals with phenomena that lie between these extremes in scope. But such variation is of considerable relevance to the assessment of evidence. This is because (other things being equal) the larger, and the greater the number of the phenomena described, the more work is required to validate the description; multiple judgements and generalisation are likely to be involved.

Descriptions of the small scale

Let us begin with the simpler case, of descriptions of single and relatively small phenomena. There are two main considerations we must bear in mind in looking at evidence for such descriptions. First, how plausible and/or credible are the evidential claims themselves? Second, how convincing is the relationship between them and the claim they have been presented to support?

Validity of evidential claims

Assessment of the validity of evidence must proceed in much the same fashion as I recommended in assessing the validity of major claims. To start with, we must assess their plausibility in terms of our existing knowledge. If they are very plausible, then we may simply accept them at face value. If not, we must assess their credibility.

In assessing credibility, we must take account of the process by which the evidential claims have been produced. The two most substantial sorts of evidence to be found in ethnographic studies are extracts from observational reports by the ethnographer and from informants' accounts.[6]

1. *The ethnographer's own observations.* These will often be presented as extracts from fieldnotes or from transcriptions of audio- or video-recordings. An example in the extract from Parker *et al.*'s research on juvenile courts is the report of an offender who had been given a fine being told that 'Perhaps, George, when your father comes out . . . er . . . comes out of prison, he'll help you pay' (p. 91). Such observations in court are presumably extracts from fieldnotes taken at the time.[7]

There are three general sources of error in observational reports that we need to consider:

(a) First, we must think about the potential effect of the research process and of the characteristics of the researcher on the behaviour observed. This is often referred to as the problem of reactivity.

In the case of Parker *et al.*'s research, I think we are reasonably safe in concluding that the researchers will have had little impact on court process; though we cannot be sure. The public nature of the events, the other constraints likely to be operating on the people involved, and the likelihood that the researchers were viewed as relatively low status, all point in this direction. However, reactivity is a problem that arises quite commonly in ethnographic research. An interesting example is provided by Pinch and Clark's study of market traders (Pinch and Clark, 1986). This research involved video-recording the sales 'spiel' of the traders, and the latter sometimes used references in their sales-talk to the researchers' camera as representing a local TV company. The researchers also acted as 'ricks' or front men/women for the traders. As Cherrington *et al.* (1987) point out in a commentary on this article, it is possible that the research process may have exaggerated certain features of the behaviour of the traders in a way that threatens the validity of findings. Of course, this problem of the research process itself affecting what is observed (what I shall call the problem of *procedural* reactivity) does not arise where the research is covert (as long as the researcher's cover is not blown). But it is always a potential problem when the people studied know they are being researched.

Equally important are the possible effects of the personal and social characteristics of the researcher on the behaviour observed; and these arise in both overt and covert research. Thus the age, gender, social class, professional identity, etc, of the researcher (or participants' perceptions of these) may affect what people do and say when being observed. The importance of the gender of the researcher has been emphasised by feminists. And while in my judgement some overemphasise the 'natural rapport' among women and exaggerate the obstacles to rapport between women and men, there is no doubt that this factor can shape research findings significantly. Age can also be important. Honigmann (1970: 62) notes how his age alienated him 'from the younger men and women, especially those deviant from the larger society's norms', in his study of an Eskimo community on Baffin

Island. Such *personal* reactivity is also an essential consideration in assessing observational reports, then; to the extent that the researcher interacts with (or is visible to) the people being studied.

Clearly, both procedural and personal reactivity can be a significant source of error in ethnographers' observations. However it is important to remember what is at issue here. It is not whether the research process or the characteristics of the researcher have affected the behaviour that was observed, but rather whether they have affected it in respects that are relevant to the claims made (and to a significant degree). Often, reactive effects may be judged likely to have occurred, but unlikely to have had a significant effect on the validity of the findings.

(b) A second source of error, as I indicated in discussing the credibility of major claims, may arise from the nature of the feature being observed. Some features (such as which pupils are allocated to which group) are less likely to be mis-perceived than others (such as the similarities or differences in treatment of groups). This is not a matter of some features being directly observed in a way that guarantees the validity of observational reports, while other features are merely inferred. All observations involve inference, but we can reasonably judge some inferences to be much more likely to be erroneous than others.

(c) Third, and equally important, we must consider the features of the researcher and of the circumstances in which the research was carried out, in so far as they might affect the validity of the ethnographer's reports. We need to think about the sorts of constraints under which observation occurred and the resulting danger of misperceiving what took place (especially when also trying to record it). Also, we must remember that fieldnotes are always selective and that where they have not been written on the spot, as is common, we must consider the possible distortions of memory. By contrast, transcripts of audio- or video-recordings have the advantage that they will usually be more accurate and fuller in reporting what was said than fieldnotes. However, they do not record everything and even transcripts are constructions: involving assumptions of various kinds, for example about who was speaking to whom (Ochs, 1979). Furthermore, what are presented in ethno-graphic accounts are *extracts* from fieldnotes or transcripts, and so we must bear in mind the process of selection at this level too, and the possible relevance of what is not quoted.

Besides features of the research process, we must also take account of what we know about the ethnographer, and the resulting potential for biases of various kinds. For instance, if we are looking at a study of political influence on the presentation of news in the mass media and we know that the researcher was commissioned by a news organisation, or (conversely) that he is a well-known critic of the media, we ought to be on the look out for the sorts of bias that are most likely in each case. Here, of course, research biographies are often an important source of information. This is not a matter of dismissing what is claimed on the grounds that the researcher is probably biased, but rather simply of taking the likely direction of bias into account in our assessment.

2. *Informants' accounts.* These may take the form of interview responses, documents of various kinds and even accounts given by one participant to another that were overheard by the researcher.

All three sources of error that I identified as operating on observers' reports must also be considered in relation to informants' accounts. Thus, in assessing them we must consider the possible effects of the informant's presence and role on what he/she observed. (Unless the informant is very closely associated with the research, the greatest danger here will be personal rather than procedural reactivity.) Second, we must assess the nature of the phenomenon being described and the implications of this for the likelihood of error. The third source of error, the reporting process itself, is more complex in the case of informants' accounts. We must note whether the account is a first-hand report on the part of the informant, or a report of what others have told the informant about what *they* saw or heard. Evidence of the latter kind is especially problematic, since we will not know what distortions may have occurred in the passage of information to the informant. It should also be borne in mind that informants are likely to rely on memory rather than fieldnotes or audio-recording, so that there is more scope for memory distortion.

In addition to assessing the threats to validity operating on the information available to the informant, we must also consider those that relate to the transmission of information from informant to ethnographer. For example, we must assess the effects of the context in which the informant's account was produced: for what audience (interviewer and/or others), in response to what stimulus, with what purposes in mind, under what constraints, etc. Also, what threats to validity may have been operative on the ethnographer's recording and interpretation of the informant's account? Such accounts may be recorded in fieldnote form or by audio-recording; and all the considerations I outlined earlier in relation to these forms of recording apply here too. Furthermore, once again, what are made available in ethnographic research reports are selections from informants' accounts, and so we must bear in mind the possible relevance of what was left out wnen we interpret the extracts presented.

Claims may also sometimes be supported by references to published sources of various kinds: whether other research reports, official documents, newspaper articles, personal diaries or autobiographies, even fictional accounts. Thus, for example, in his discussion of Edinburgh medical students' judgements of clinical units, Atkinson appeals for support to Becker and Geer's study of local medical student culture in a North American hospital (Atkinson, 1981a: 23; Becker *et al.* 1961). And earlier, in his discussion of the division of preclinical and clinical phases of medical education and the malaise it can cause among students, he cites the report of the Royal Commission on Medical Education (Atkinson, 1981a: 17). Elsewhere, he draws on a novel by Richard Gordon to illustrate the nature of bedside teaching (Atkinson, 1975). References to published sources can be used both as a basis for inferences about the features of their author(s) and as accounts telling us about the phenomena to which they refer. That is, they may be used in ways analogous both to observers' reports and to informants' accounts.[8]

How much reliance we place on such published evidence involves difficult judgements. After all, it may involve all the sorts of potential threat to validity that apply to any research report. And we should remember that authors' references to sources are not always accurate. Our judgement should depend greatly on the nature of the source itself (as far as we can judge this) and the purpose for which it is being used. It may sometimes be necessary to examine the source for ourselves.

Another sort of evidence that may be provided in support of descriptions (and sometimes also explanations) is what is sometimes referred to as respondent validation. Here the ethnographer's account is presented to the people (or more usually to some of the people) to whom it refers, and their judgements about its validity reported. Sometimes this seems to be taken as the litmus test of validity in ethnographic research (see, for example, Lincoln and Guba, 1985). However, while such evidence is of value, it cannot be treated as providing a definitive test of validity unless we assume that participants both know (or can recognise) for certain the relevant facts about their situation and behaviour *and* are able and willing to admit such facts. There seem to me to be no good reasons for adopting either of these assumptions in a blanket fashion. Whether they are reasonable will depend on the nature of the claim and of the participant and her or his circumstances. The same approach should be applied to such data as to all informant accounts, it seems to me. And in no circumstances can participant responses be taken as absolutely certain evidence for either the truth or the falsity of claims.

A useful form of check on the validity of descriptive claims that ethnographers sometimes employ is triangulation. This can take a variety of forms, but the principle involved is simple. If we accept that all kinds of data involve potential threats to validity, and that these may differ in likelihood across data types and sources, then by comparing data carrying different validity threats we may be able to make a more effective assessment of the likely truth of the claim. Explicit examples of triangulation are rare in ethnographic studies. One example, though, is provided by Lever (1981), arising from her research on sex differences in children's play, where she compares questionnaire and diary data. What is hoped for in triangulation, of course, is that the different data sources will confirm one another. But frequently this does not happen. For example, Lever found that the questionnaire data showed stronger sex differences in play activities than did the diary reports. Faced with such a discrepancy, the researcher and the reader must try to make some assessment of the reasons for it so that a conclusion can be reached about which finding is most likely to be true. Lever argues that the discrepancy in her study arose from the fact that questionnaire data probably tend to elicit responses that are more influenced by a person's perceptions of social norms than are diary entries; and so she concludes that the latter are the more accurate. As readers, we must consider the plausibility of this argument, both in itself and in comparison with others that point in a different direction. For example, might it be the case that the diary entries covered a shorter period of time and were not representative of the usual patterns; whereas the questionnaire data drew on the children's own greater experience of what they typically do? It should be noted that such issues arise even where the different data sources confirm one another. We must ask whether these sources might have shared some common source of error that would explain their similar results and indicate that they may both be wrong.

In this section I have considered assessment of the validity of evidential claims in their own terms. Equally important, though, is whether and how strongly they support the major claims for which they are used as evidence.

The relationship between evidence and claim

The evidence may seem quite plausible and/or credible in itself, and yet the support it offers for the claim may be questionable. Take, for example, the following extract dealing with the adaptations of female factory workers to their work:

'Cutting off', or separating, the 'inner self' from what is objectively happening on the 'outside' is one of the sorry 'skills' we are forced into, in an existence dominated by alienated relations of production. It is otherwise known as 'wishing one's life away'. Some girls actually prided themselves in the art of switching off, pitying those who were bad at it, and thinking themselves lucky to be working at all:

> Racquel: Yes, you get bored sitting up here, very bored... You gets used to it, though. I think it's imagination a lot of the time. I get fed up sometimes, but I don't really get that fed up, because I haven't really got anything to be fed up about.
>
> Anna (the researcher): What do you think about?
>
> Racquel: Nothing, really. I can sit up here a whole day without really speaking.

(Pollert, 1981: 131)

Here the evidence offered takes the form of an informant's account of her life at work. It is not clear whether the extract is from fieldnotes or from audio-recording, but either way there is no obvious reason to doubt that it is an accurate representation of what was said. However, a serious question does arise about the relationship of this evidence to the multiple claims the author makes in the discussion that precedes the quotation. These claims are:

1. that the workers cut themselves off or switch off from their work;
2. that they refer to this as 'wishing one's life away'; and that it is a 'sorry' skill produced by alienated relations of production;
3. that some of the women prided themselves on their ability to switch off, and pitied those who were bad at it, judging themselves lucky to be working.

The quotation supports the first claim (assuming that this worker is typical of the rest). However, it provides no evidence for the other two claims. What this indicates is that we must look carefully at the relationship between evidence and claims: evidence sometimes gives only partial support for the set of claims that the author is presenting.

Sometimes, too, one finds that there are alternative plausible interpretations of the evidence that would not support the claim. Take the following example, also from Pollert's study. Here the evidence quoted below is intended to support the argument that 'supervision was sexually oppressive' and that the women were forced into a 'defensive–aggressive strategy' on the men's terms:

> On one occasion one of the (. . .) girls was 'messing around' and was wheeled off to a lift on a trolley by a young man. Everybody joined in the joke:
>
> Kathy: It weren't my fault. (*Shrieking*)
>
> Steven (Chargehand): What are you up to? It's your sexy looks that always does it.

Brenda: (looking on, and giving a husky laugh): Watch him back there! Oh! – I wouldn't trust *him*!

There was no way the chargehand could have broken up the general 'laugh' without antagonising the girls. So he diffused it with jocular flattery, never even approaching the young man who was responsible. The girl returned to work, put in her place; but instead of sheepishly acknowledging his authority, was able to continue giggling, as if to demonstrate she did not feel humiliated. (Pollert, 1981: 143)

It is possible that this is indeed an example of sexual oppression, and that the participation of the women was 'a defensive–aggressive strategy' on the men's terms that they were 'forced into'. Clearly Pollert is drawing on considerable experience of life in the factory she describes. However, I do not find this evidence to be convincing support for her claim. There are elements of it which suggest a different, equally plausible interpretation. There is no clear indication that the men started this incident or that they transformed what had already begun into something else. While the author suggests that 'the young man' was responsible, it is not clear on what basis this judgement was made; and given this I think we must suspend judgement about it. Furthermore, Pollert reports that 'everyone joined in the joke' and that it was a 'general laugh' which the chargehand could not have broken up without antagonising the girls. These features might be taken to suggest a process of joking around that both sexes found congenial, especially as a break from work. Pollert claims that the woman was 'put in her place' and humiliated by the chargehand, and that her response was designed to disguise this. But this is an especially difficult sort of interpretation to establish. We cannot assume that all women would always be humiliated by such 'jocular flattery'. No doubt some would, in some circumstances. But what evidence is there to suggest that this is a case in point. This is not the kind of description that one can read off from an observation with minimal danger of misinterpretation. At the very least, some account from the women involved in this incident is required. An additional problem is that it is not even very clear what would count as sexual oppression, neither the intension nor extension of this concept are well defined. While core examples are fairly obvious, the boundaries are unclear; and this example is outside that core, it seems to me. Furthermore, much to her credit, Pollert makes her own feminist views quite explicit at the beginning of her book (Pollert, 1981: 2). Given these views, and presuming that they predated the research, we can suspect that she may have been predisposed to find such oppression. This might lead her to detect examples that others, such as non-feminists and men, would miss. Equally, though, it might also lead her to misinterpret some incidents as sexually oppressive that were not. As readers we have to make a judgement on the evidence that she provides, and our judgements will of course reflect our own views and experience to some degree. What is essential, though, is that we strive to find common ground for such judgements, and for me Pollert does not succeed in finding it in this case.[9]

The problem of the relationship between evidence and claim may also arise where appeal is made to published sources. For example, when Parker *et al.* appeal to a national study of magistrates to support their claim about the middle-class background of magistrates at Countyside (Parker *et al.* 1981:89), we must ask whether we can be confident about inferring from the findings of that study to the situation at Countyside. The relationship may turn out to be convincing, but the issue must be addressed.

Description of larger scale phenomena

Let us now broaden our focus to look at descriptions of larger geographical and/or temporal phenomena that cannot be observed by an ethnographer or informant in one go. Here the claim (explicitly or implicitly) will involve a synthesis of multiple judgements and probably also generalisation from what was observed to what was not. Most claims in ethnographic research reports are of this kind; indeed, many of those discussed in the previous section fall into this category. Often there are generalisations across a population of participants in a setting, as when Parker *et al.* make claims about all or most of the magistrates working in Countyside Court on the basis of evidence presented about the attitudes and actions of a few of them. Simultaneously, there may also be generalisation over time, so that Parker *et al.*'s claim that magistrates at Countyside espoused a criminal family thesis was not a claim about what magistrates believed at one brief point in time but rather about what was assumed to be a stable feature of their behaviour over the whole period of observation, and perhaps beyond.

Sometimes such generalisation is plausible or credible at face value, but often we may need evidence to establish that what is true of the instance described is likely to be true of others within the case. And where such evidence is not available we must suspend judgement. Thus, it seems to me that Parker *et al.* do not establish that all or even a majority of Countyside magistrates were committed to the criminal families thesis, nor that it was a stable feature of their orientation over time.

Sometimes generalisations within the case studied may be supported by data about multiple instances, including reports about the precise frequency of the relevant events. This may take the form of information about the frequency with which a particular sort of opinion was expressed across a population of informants. Equally, it may be a report about the frequency of the relevant sort of event over time. An example of the latter is to be found in Pollard's study of the effects of classroom regime on the differentiation of pupils. He argues that traditional forms of teaching tend to result in friendships among children being correlated with academic achievement levels. In seeking to document the differences in teaching style between the two teachers he studied Pollard provides a table that reports the frequency of different sorts of contact between them and their pupils.

Table 1   *Teacher–child contacts %*

| | Child intitiated | | Teacher initiated | | |
	Work related	*Other*	*Work related*	*Other*	*Advisory*
Mrs Rothwell's class	12	15	27	11	35
Mr Harman's class	20	32	18	17	13

(Adapted from Pollard 1984, p. 36)

It is certainly of great value to have evidence of this kind. It provides much more of a basis on which to judge the soundness of the generalisation than where the writer simply asserts that such and such frequently happened or was generally true. However, this evidence must still be handled carefully; questions may need to be asked about it. In the case of Pollard's data, there are things we need to know:

(a) What was the period over which the observation of teacher–pupil contacts was carried out? Was it continuous? What was its size relative to the time-span over which generalisation is being made?

(b) How rigorously were teacher–child contacts identified? Variations in identification procedure over the course of observation are a potential source of error and we need to know how large this error might be. This covers both the question of how clear and concrete the identification criteria were and how effectively, practically speaking, these criteria were applied. For example, was the coding done on the spot in the classroom or on the basis of a video-recording? This might make a difference to the level of error. On the one hand, video-recording might reduce the likelihood of error in recording the data; on the other, it may suggest a higher level of procedural reactivity.

(c) How rigorously were the child/teacher initiative and work-related/other/advisory distinctions made? Again, we need to know how closely specified the categories were and how effective the counting of instances was, given practical constraints.

Numerical frequencies should not be taken as self-evident proof of generalisability, then. While they provide us with more of a basis for assessing generalisations across people and/or over time than mere assertions about frequencies, threats to their validity must still be addressed.

In this section I have looked at the assessment of descriptions, both of small and of larger scale phenomena. This requires examining the plausibility and/or credibility of the claims and of any evidence provided in their support. In the case of evidence, we must look at both the likely validity of the evidential claims themselves and of the inferences from evidence back to claim. Finally, I looked at the problem of generalising within the case, the sorts of evidence that are used to support such generalisations and the considerations that must be borne in mind in assessing them.

EXPLANATIONS AND PREDICTIONS

As I noted in Chapter 2, all types of claim (except definitions) include a descriptive component. Given this, a first step in assessing the validity of explanatory and predictive claims is to identify and assess their component descriptions, explicit or implicit. This is done in precisely the same way as one assesses any other description. Over and above this, though, we must look at how well the evidence supports the specifically explanatory or predictive element of the claim. There are two steps in this process. First, all explanations and predictions involve theoretical assumptions and it is necessary to assess the validity of these. Second, it must be shown that the explanation or prediction fits the case at least as well as any competing alternative.

An example

To illustrate the assessment of explanations I want to look again at the extract from Parker *et al.*'s study of juvenile courts that I discussed in Chapter 2. You may remember that their aim in that extract was to explain why the sentencing in Countyside Court was more punitive than at City Court. They argue that this cannot be simply because there was a social-class differential between magistrates and offenders. The critical factor, they argue, was the relative absence of institutionalised procedures within Countyside Court that would have minimised the effects of the inappropriate, social class-based assumptions held by magistrates, as they did at City Court. I shall look first at the descriptive claims involved in this argument, and then at assessment of the explanatory element.

Descriptive claims

There are several descriptive claims involved in this explanation:

(a) that justice at Countyside Court is punitive/more harsh than at City Court;
(b) that there is a sharp social-class differential between magistrates and offenders in both courts;
(c) that the court officials' assumption that there was an underclass of criminal families in Countyside was false;
(d) that procedures of 'due process', etc., were less operative at Countyside than at City Court.

Descriptive claim (a). This is the description of the phenomenon to be explained. As we noted earlier, it is slightly ambiguous. It looks like a value claim: that justice at Countyside is unfair. And, indeed, I think it does have this character. However, it is also factual: it implies that cases of the same sort incurred more severe sentences at Countyside than at City. And this forms the basis for a major claim of the book as a whole:

(. . .) we find that juveniles from the same backgrounds (. . .), charged with similar offences, are subjected to quite different court regimes, and receive widely divergent sentences, which have major and wide-ranging effects on their lives. (Parker *et al.*, 1981: 22)

For the moment I shall restrict consideration to the factual element of the claim that sentencing at Countyside is more harsh than at City Court. Clearly, it is not an argument that is immediately convincing in itself: it is not so plausible that we do not need to consider its credibility. Nor, in my judgement, is it credible as it stands, since it involves the comparison of individual cases with respect to the defendants' backgrounds, the offences committed and the relative severity of the sentences handed down. Furthermore, I think we need evidence about the validity of the generalisation from the cases discussed to all those occurring at Countyside in the relevant period.

Parker *et al.* do provide some evidence for this claim in the extract included in Chapter 2, though it is not explicitly presented for this purpose. They claim that 'Fines tend to be comparatively high', and they report two instances of the use of compensation orders that they regard as severe (see p. 34 above).

The first of these evidential claims involves generalisation and comparison (presumably with City Court), but the basis for neither is indicated. In my judgement, the complex nature of this claim means that it cannot be accepted without further supporting evidence; and none is provided.

The other two items of evidence are more specific. For the most part I think that we can accept the validity of the evidence itself. The only exception is the suggestion that 'because the presiding magistrates went out of their way to state, quite unsolicited, that the compensation had absolutely nothing to do with the car being a Daimler' we can infer that the make of car *did* have an effect on the level of compensation.[10] We are all aware that people do not always tell the truth, and are not even always aware of their own motivations; and this seems as likely to be true of magistrates as of anyone else. However, when we take what people say as implying the converse, we must surely provide evidence. Since the authors offer no evidence, I think we must suspend judgement about the validity of this particular argument. The rest of the evidence, however, seems credible at face value.

More problematic is the relationship between this evidence and the claim that these two cases are instances of relatively punitive justice. As with the general statement about the comparatively high level of fines, here too issues of comparison and generalisation are involved for which we need evidence; and, again, none is provided.

Earlier in their book Parker *et al.* provide some other evidence for the claim that justice at Countyside is comparatively punitive, in the form of data on the proportions of various types of disposal at Countyside compared with City Court, all courts in the same metropolitan region and all juvenile courts in England and Wales. I have summarised these data in Figure 2, which clearly shows that the proportion of more severe sentences (detention centre and borstal recommendation) is higher at Countyside Court than elsewhere. This is certainly stronger evidence than that available in the extract, and provides a useful complement to it. However, there are reasons why even this evidence could be misleading. For instance, there may be something about the cases that Countyside Court deals with that explains the different profile of disposals there. Are there more recidivists, or are the offences typically more serious, etc.? Indeed, if the Countyside magistrates were right and there was an underclass of criminal families in their area, but not in City, then this might explain the deviant pattern of disposals at Countyside. This is such an important claim in the context of Parker *et al.*'s study that I think we need more information before we can make a reasonable judgement.

Descriptive claim (b). This second claim relates to one of the factors held to explain the punitive character of justice at Countyside. And it seems to me that the argument that there is a social-class differential between magistrates and defendants is quite plausible as it stands. On the basis of everyday knowledge I think we can accept that the magistrates at Countyside were probably middle class and that since the working class are disproportionately represented among defendants in juvenile courts this was probably the case at Countyside. These seem reasonable conclusions, despite their probabilistic character and the vagueness of the terms 'middle class' and 'working class'. The authors do offer some evidence in support of this claim and this adds further to the claim's plausibility.

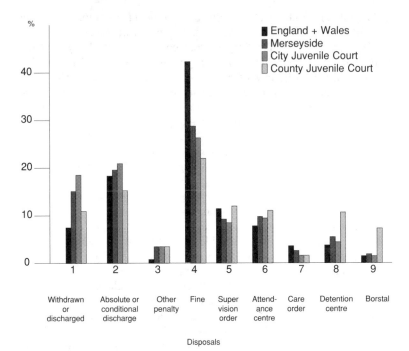

Figure 2 *Means of disposal of all juveniles (10–17 yrs) proceeded against as percentages of all cases dealt with for indictable and non-indictable offences (1978/1979)*

(Constructed from Table 5.1, p79 in Parker et al 1981)

Descriptive claim (c). We cannot accept this claim as plausible or credible at face value, but the authors do provide some evidence. They test the criminal families thesis against information about the frequency with which the same names recurred on the Countyside juvenile court records over the year during which they carried out their observations. From this they conclude that the thesis was false. However, in my view a year is likely to be too short a time to pick up a pattern of recurring names. Five or six years might have been a more convincing test. I think we have to suspend judgement about the validity of this claim.

Descriptive claim (d). This claim refers to what the authors take to be the key element in the explanation of the punitive character of Countyside justice. It is a comparative claim about the relationship between proceedings in City and Countyside Courts. Elsewhere in their book, the authors describe the legal process in City Court as characterised by operational but unwritten rules that have become normative over time, having the following three features:

(i) due process is adhered to most of the time and even on those occasions when it was deviated from this did not seem to go against the offenders' interests.[11] Thus, court personnel took great care to explain the charge and to elicit the correct plea by talking to both juvenile and parent(s). 70% of offenders had legal representation and this was encouraged, only 4% of applications for legal aid were refused.

(ii) civil treatment of offenders and their families was the norm.

(iii) the full tariff of sentences was used, usually proceeding up the ladder of severity of disposal one step at a time.

(Parker *et al.*, 1981: ch. 4)

By contrast, the authors claim that at Countyside Court due process was more frequently 'interpreted', either to serve the interests of court personnel or 'to inflict moral or social stigma upon defendants and parents'. Thus there was 'not much attempt to explain jargon and check that the defendant understood what is going on' (Parker *et al.*, 1981: 82). Defendants and their families were 'herded' into court and the charge read without much allowance for questions. Also, there was a failure to offer defendants basic courtesy, and extraneous material was introduced that was insulting and stigmatising. Furthermore, Countyside Court tended to accept a defendant's desire to proceed without legal representation rather than urging the desirability of representation; and it refused a higher level of applications for legal aid than did City. There was also a failure to give reasons, either for the refusal of aid or for the sentences given. Finally, Countyside Court magistrates used a short tariff, moving quite quickly to severe punishments (Parker *et al.*, 1981: ch. 5)

This claim and its components cannot be accepted as sufficiently plausible at face value; nor is its credibility sufficient, since multiple and comparative judgements are involved as well as generalisations over time. We require evidence, I think. The authors recognise this and provide a considerable amount of evidence in support of this claim. For the most part, though, this is concerned with the attitudes of the magistrates and court officials as these are revealed by what is said and done in court (and in interviews); rather than with showing that due process was not adhered to, and that magistrates did not make use of the full tariff. What this evidence does support, to some degree, is that officials were sometimes uncivil to defendants and to their parents; though even here we are given little contextual information by which we can check this interpretation, and it is not clear how representative of court process at Countyside such examples of incivility were.

Explanatory claims

Where, as in this case, we have found one or more of the descriptive claims involved in an explanation to be unconvincing the explanation as a whole cannot be convincing. However, it is still worth considering the level of conviction that we should have in the explanatory component of Parker *et al.*'s argument. The explanation that these authors put forward has two links:

a) that the social class background of City and Countyside magistrates gives them false (or otherwise inappropriate) assumptions about defendants and their families;

b) that the relative absence of institutionalised procedures implementing due process etc. led to these inappropriate assumptions influencing court decisions and thereby producing relatively punitive justice at Countyside.

Explanatory claim (a).[12] In assessing the explanatory component of claims we must begin by considering the theoretical assumption on which it is based. Here, the general idea seems to be that people's social-class background affects how they see the world and may lead to erroneous views about the lives of people in other social classes. In my judgement this is quite plausible enough to accept as a theoretical principle. As regards its plausibility as an explanation of events at Countyside, we should note that we have accepted that there does seem likely to have been a social-class differential between magistrates and defendants there, so that the conditions for the application of this theoretical principle are met. On the other hand, we saw that the claim that the magistrates' attitudes were false and inappropriate had not been established. Furthermore, the validity of this explanation in relation to alternatives is not assessed. And the claim that the criminal families thesis and other attitudes that Countyside magistrates display are characteristically middle class is not entirely convincing. Age or generation might be factors of at least equal importance. This first explanatory argument is not entirely convincing, then.

Explanatory claim (b). The theoretical assumption presupposed by this explanation seems to be that unless constrained by institutional procedures, inappropriate assumptions about others will result in relatively severe treatment of them (compared to people of one's own class or group). This also seems reasonably plausible. We are all aware of how ethnocentrism of one kind or another can blind us to the problems that other people face, and so lead us to unfair treatment. Once again, though, we must ask whether it seems likely *in this case* that the phenomena being explained would not have occurred if the explanatory factor cited had not been present. My major doubt about this explanation concerns the question of why the institutionalised procedures operated at City but not at Countyside. This is especially important because it seems plausible that the relative weakness of institutionalised procedures and the severe sentencing at Countyside could both have been products of some other factor, rather than the former causing the latter.

Predictions

Summary

What this discussion suggests, I think, is that we need a good deal more evidence before we should be convinced that Parker *et al.*'s explanatory argument is valid. However, whether or not you agree with this judgement, I hope that the discussion has given you a sense of what I take to be involved in assessing explanatory claims. As I suggested earlier, we cannot expect that there will always be a consensus in judgements about validity, not even after detailed discussion; but this does not deny the possibility of rational assessment or that consensus *can* often be reached.

A similar sort of approach is required in assessing predictions. These are less common than explanations in ethnographic accounts, and for this reason I shall not give them as much attention. We must, of course, begin by assessing the description of the situation or causal factor from which the predicted event is believed likely to stem; and (if the period over which the prediction should have been fulfilled has expired) we must examine any account of what actually occurred and its relationship to what was predicted. The next concern, as with explanations, is the validity of the theoretical assumption(s) on which the prediction is based. Can we accept it (or them) as plausible? Finally, we must consider the possibility that the predicted event would have occurred even if the factor which is claimed to have produced it had not happened, or that some other factor explains both of them. Here again we must rely on thought experiments to assess the likelihood of different outcomes under varying conditions.

The assessment of explanations and predictions, then, involves all the considerations that I outlined in discussing descriptions, plus distinctive issues concerning the specifically explanatory or predictive element. The latter, like the former, requires us to make judgements about what is plausible and credible, judgements that can be reasonable or unreasonable but whose validity or invalidity we can never know with absolute certainty.

EVALUATIONS AND PRESCRIPTIONS

In assessing evidence for value claims, once again we begin with their descriptive components. Is the phenomenon evaluated, or the situation to be rectified by the prescribed policy, accurately represented? In addition to this, in the case of prescriptions a predictive assumption is also involved: that if such and such a course of action were to be taken a particular type of situation would result. The validity of such assumptions must also be assessed.

The distinctively evaluative or prescriptive element of claims concerns whether the phenomenon described, or the situation the policy prescribes, is good or bad. We must decide whether evidence is required to support this component, and if so, of what kind. As we saw in the previous chapter, the idea of assessing the validity of value claims is a controversial one, but I outlined there the basis on which I believe that it can be done legitimately: by appeal to what are likely to be widely accepted value and factual assumptions; and recourse to common ground where disagreement arises. On this basis, we must consider both what values have and have not been, should and should not have been, taken into account in the value judgement; and how those values have been interpeted in their application to the particular phenomena concerned. I shall discuss this in the context of evaluations, since these are more common and usually more central than prescriptions in ethnographic research.

As an illustration of how one might set about assessing evaluations in ethnographic research, let me return again to the study of juvenile courts by Parker *et al.*. In its overall conception, this was an explicitly evaluative study. The authors were concerned to test the quality of the justice dispensed by City and Countyside Courts. I have already dealt with the descriptive and explanatory components of their argument, so I shall concentrate here on the evaluative element. To begin with we must ask what values underly their evaluation. Fairly obviously, the key value is justice, but several aspects of this value are mentioned by the authors. First, this value is taken to imply that, in formal terms, there should be consistency of treatment within the same court over time and between courts, so that the same sorts of cases are treated in the same way. Second, the authors distinguish between two bases on which judgements about the equivalence of cases can be made; and they advocate one of these over the other. On the one hand, natural justice involves taking account of such things as the seriousness of the offence and the previous record of the defendant, abstracting the offender and offence from the rest of their social context. What the authors call 'social justice', on the other hand, takes account of some of the social (including material) circumstances of the offender so that, for example, family poverty might be a basis for mitigating sentences where it was judged the contributory factor to the offence. The first of these standards of assessment (consistency of treatment) seems acceptable as it stands and therefore not in need of justification. The second, advocacy of social justice, is more controversial. While it is certainly not an unreasonable concept, it is not the one that is institutionalised in the courts, and it has been the subject of debate. Given this, we need some supporting argument as to why it is preferable to natural justice. And part of that discussion should probably deal with the problems that might arise if that concept of justice were adopted by the courts, and how those problems could be dealt with. For example, how would magistrates assess poverty and what degree of mitigation should be involved? Parker *et al.* provide some justificatory argument in support of the concept of social justice, though in my view they do not deal with all the questions that require treatment (Parker, *et al.*, 1981: 246–7).

Parker *et al.*'s study is fairly unusual among ethnographic accounts in its openness about its evaluative goal, and in the degree to which it makes the values relied on explicit and seeks to justify them. More commonly, evaluations are introduced in the course of descriptions and explanations without being clearly signalled and the values on which they are based remain implicit. Sometimes this causes no problems, since the values are easily identifiable and plausible. Often, though, the basis for the evaluation is neither clear nor obviously justifiable (see, for instance, Hammersley 1990b).

ASSESSING THE CONCLUSIONS DRAWN

In Chapter 2, I drew a distinction between the main claims of an ethnographic account (which relate to the case studied) and the conclusions drawn on the basis of those claims (which relate to the focus of the research). Sometimes, there may be no separate focus, and therefore no conclusions beyond the main claims. Most ethnographic studies, though, do draw such conclusions. Thus, having assessed the main arguments of the study, we shall often have to give separate consideration to its conclusions. Usually, what this will involve is assessing the basis on which inferences from claim to conclusion were made. In Chapter 2 I identified two strategies by which ethnographers seek to draw such inferences: theoretical inference and empirical generalisation. Here I want to look at how we assess examples of each of these types of inference.

Theoretical inference

Theoretical claims are distinctive in that they are universal in scope: they refer to a range of possible cases (those where the conditions are met) rather than specifically to a finite set of actual cases. What we must assess in the case of theoretical concerns is the extent to which evidence about the case(s) studied can provide a basis for such universal claims.

We should begin by recognising that there is one sense in which no basis for universal claims can be provided: evidence about a finite number of particular cases can never allow us to draw conclusions on a strictly logical basis (that is, with complete certainty) about a universal. This is known as the problem of induction. Various attempts have been made to find some logical basis for induction, but it is widely agreed that none of these has been successful (Popper, 1959; Black, 1967; Newton-Smith, 1981). However, once we abandon the idea that a claim to validity must be certain beyond all possible doubt before we can call it knowledge, and accept that we can distinguish between claims that are more or less likely to be true, the problem of induction becomes less severe (though still not easy to deal with). In short, once we adopt a subtle realism we can, in principle at least, draw reasonable conclusions about theoretical claims.

One of the problems with the concept of theoretical inference is that it has been interpreted in several (often not clearly distinguished) ways by ethnographers (Hammersley, 1989b and 1990c). The approach that has been most fully explicated in the literature on ethnographic method is the idea that by studying critical cases we can draw inferences about the truth or falsity of theories. This is sometimes referred to as analytic induction (Znaniecki, 1934; Lindesmith, 1937 and 1968; Cressey, 1953).

Cressey's study of embezzlement is one of the best examples of this approach. His central question was: Under what conditions do people take the decision to embezzle? In developing and testing his theory Cressey studied a large number of cases, interviewing people who had been convicted of embezzlement and other forms of 'financial trust violation'. His final formulation was that:

Trusted persons become trust violators when they conceive of themselves as having a financial problem which is non-shareable, have the knowledge or awareness that this problem can be secretly resolved by violation of the position of financial trust, and are able to apply to their own conduct in that situation verbalizations that enable them to adjust their conceptions of themselves as trusted persons with their conceptions of themselves as users of the entrusted funds or property. (Cressey 1950: 742)

During the course of his research Cressey reformulated his theory several times in the face of falsifying evidence. And it does seem highly plausible. However, it is important to notice that cases were selected for investigation on the basis that they exhibited the phenomenon the theory was designed to explain (embezzlement). As Robinson (1951) points out, at best this research strategy can identify only factors that are *necessary* for embezzlement to occur; it cannot identify factors that are *sufficient* to bring it about. This is because there was no investigation of cases where the factors assumed to cause embezzlement were present to discover whether it always (or more frequently) occurred in those cases.

What this suggests is that research concerned with developing and testing theory must seek to identify both necessary *and* sufficient conditions, and therefore requires that we investigate cases where the theoretical variable takes contrasting values, with a view to finding out if the phenomenon being explained varies in the way that the theory would lead us to expect. Also required is that the cases should be such that relevant extraneous variables (those which might also produce the phenomenon being investigated) are controlled (that is, kept at the same level or minimised). These features are largely absent from Cressey's study.[13] The only ethnographic research of which I am aware that approximates this model is the series of studies by Hargreaves, Lacey, and Ball. This research involved the development and testing of differentiation-polarisation theory: the claim that differentiation of pupils on academic-behavioural grounds produces polarisation in their attitudes towards school.[14]

This sequence of studies began with an investigation of a secondary modern school, where the researcher can have had little doubt that polarisation of attitudes would be found. Differentiation-polarisation theory was presented as applying to processes in the school at two levels. First, at the organisational level, it was claimed that the streaming of the pupils produced a polarisation in their perspectives between top and bottom streams (the former predominantly pro-school, the latter predominantly anti-school), with the middle two streams occupying an intermediate position. Second, it was suggested that differentiation *within* classes produced intra-class polarisation of attitude, with those placed at the top of the class being pro-school and those at the bottom anti-school. Hargreaves uses a simple diagram to illustrate the combined effect of these two differentiation-polarisation processes:

I shall focus on differentiation-polarisation theory as it applies at the organisational level, since this is the form in which the theory has been developed most effectively. In these terms, what Hargreaves' study amounts to is the description of a case where differentiation was high and so too was polarisation. Useful though this is, it is obviously rather weak evidence for the validity of the theory. After all, many other factors were likely to have been operative in the situation, some of which may well have produced the high level of polarisation. For instance, perhaps the streaming system in the school Hargreaves studied sorted pupils on the basis of their attitudes to school, these being largely a product of extra-school factors. This could have occurred both directly because this was judged to be an important consideration by teachers, and indirectly because attitude affected pupils' academic performance. Differences in pupil attitude produced by factors outside the school could therefore explain the correlation between stream and orientation to school that Hargreaves found.

4A   4B   4C   4D

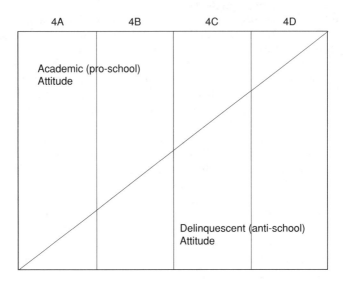

Academic (pro-school)
Attitude

Delinquescent (anti-school)
Attitude

(From Hargreaves, 1967: 163)

Figure 3 *Representation of two subcultures*

If we turn now to Lacey's study of a grammar school, we can see how it contributes to the process of testing the theory. Not only does he document much the same correlation between stream and attitude as Hargreaves, but:

1. The case he studied involved some control over the factor of differences between pupils in attitude on entry to the school. This is because Hightown was a selective school, so most of the pupils who were recruited to it had been successful and highly motivated in their primary schools.
2. He shows that the polarisation increased over time from the point of initial differentiation in the first year through to the fourth year of secondary schooling.

This certainly adds considerably to the plausibility of the theory, in my judgement. Of course, it does not render it completely convincing, beyond all possible doubt. As regards the first feature of Lacey's study, we might argue that differences in attitude are a matter of degree, so that they will still exist and could have an effect even among grammar school pupils. Thus, the streaming system at Hightown may simply have allocated pupils to streams on the basis of differences in attitude among new recruits, despite the fact that these differences were small compared with those to be found across the whole age group. Similarly, we might seek to explain the growing polarisation over time not as the product of differentiation but as the result of external factors operating on existing differences in attitude. After all, a lot of things happen to pupils during their secondary school careers, both changes in relationships at home and in peer groups; and some of these are likely to be systematically related to attitude towards school.[15] It is in the nature of all theory-testing, especially in non-experimental research, that there will often be other factors that might plausibly explain the findings.

In the third of this sequence of studies, Ball investigated a comprehensive school. As a result of this choice of school type he was not able to control for pupils' attitude on entry in the way that Lacey did. However, he did look at change in pupils' attitudes over time, confirming Lacey's findings. Furthermore, he was able to document a change in the level of differentiation in the institution (the abandonment of banding in favour of mixed ability grouping), looking at the effects of this on the level of polarisation. Given that this involved a change within a single institution we can assume that much (though not everything) remained the same between the two situations, before and after.[16] Ball shows that the level of polarisation was much lower after mixed ability grouping had been adopted.

This is further important evidence in support of differentiation-polarisation theory, but once again it is not beyond reasonable question. It does not rule out all the other relevant possibilities. For example, the data produced by these studies could be explained by a kind of imitation theory whereby the attitudes of members of a school class are affected by the balance of extant pro- and anti-school attitudes to be found within it, a theory that some teachers hold. This would explain the reduction of polarisation following the abolition of banding independently of level of differentiation.[17]

Whatever the remaining questions, this sequence of studies is one of the clearest examples of systematic theory development and testing in ethnographic research, and indeed in sociology generally. It illustrates what is required but rarely done; and as such it provides a standard against which we can compare studies that claim to draw theoretical conclusions.

As we saw in Chapter 2, ethnographic studies do often claim that the case studied is crucial for some theory. However, sometimes the theory involved is not well defined (being mixed up with descriptive and explanatory arguments) and the critical character of the case is not clearly established. Woods' work on course choice in a secondary school, and the effects of examination pressure on this, involves a much clearer specification of why the case studied is of critical importance for the theory than is commonly found in ethnographic research (see Chapter 2; Woods, 1979a and b). Even here, though, there are problems. First, he does not provide evidence to establish the critical nature of the case: comparatively speaking, how heavy was the pressure on this school to achieve good examination results? If the school was not distinctive in this respect, and other schools under greater pressure gave greater choice, this would throw doubt on the theory. Second, Woods does not give attention to other factors that might have produced limited course choice for pupils. Perhaps because of a rather traditional orientation the teachers had never been committed to giving pupils a wide range of choice? Perhaps resource limitations were very severe and this limited choice? etc.

It is worth reiterating, though, that there are problems with the very notion of theory. Few ethnographers today believe that universal laws of human behaviour exist. They argue that human actions are not causally determined, or at least not fully determined, and do not conform to lawlike patterns (Blumer, 1939 and 1969; Matza, 1964 and 1969). If this is true, the strategy I outlined above is not an appropriate model for theoretical inference. And on this basis some would deny that studies like those of Cressey and Hargreaves/Lacey/Ball produce either new theoretical ideas or ideas that are more precise or better established than those which are routinely used in sociological explanations. Yet it is not clear what the alternative to this approach is.

Empirical generalisation

This is the other way in which ethnographers may seek to draw conclusions about their research focus from their findings about the case studied. Here the aim is to generalise from the case(s) studied to some larger whole or aggregate of cases of which it forms part. A first requirement in assessing such generalisations is to know the identity of the larger aggregate. As I noted in Chapter 2, this is not always made explicit by authors. Similarly, it is not always clear on what grounds the author believes that the case(s) studied are typical of the larger population. In the absence of such information the reader must try to judge what the most likely population is, and consider the likely validity of generalisation to that population on this basis.

It is important not to see statistical sampling techniques as the only way in which empirical generalisations can be made.[18] It is very rare that these techniques can be used in ethnographic research since the ratio of cases to the size of the population is not usually large enough. However, there are sorts of evidence that ethnographers can use to support empirical generalisation. Thus, it may be possible to draw on relevant information in published statistics about the aggregate to which generalisation is being made. So, while Parker *et al.* used statistics about the proportions of different sorts of disposal in juvenile courts in England and Wales and the Merseyside area to show the atypicality of Countyside, these data also establish the relative typicality (in this respect) of City Court. Similarly, where other studies have been carried out on other cases in the same population in the same time period comparison may allow some judgement of typicality to be made. An example is provided by Strong in his study of paediatric consultations. He argues that the bureaucratic format he identified is not just typical of such consultations in the National Health Service but also that (with minor modifications) it predominates in all medical consultations in the British health service. In order to establish this he first considers the extent to which the fact that children were the patients in the paediatric consultations he studied shaped the ceremonial order characteristic of them, arguing that it made little difference. Second, he draws on other studies of medical consultation involving adults as patients to assess how far these conformed to the bureaucratic mode.

In Chapter 2 I noted that the atypicality of the case studied was sometimes used as a basis for generalising to some larger population, citing the example of Cicourel and Kitsuse's study of Lakeshore High (Cicourel and Kitsuse 1973). The paradoxical character of this strategy is only superficial. While Cicourel and Kitsuse declare Lakeside High to be atypical of other US high schools (at the time the research was carried out), they claim that it is typical (in relevant respects) of how US high schools will be in the future. The same considerations apply to this as to more conventional forms of generalisation. The only difference is that since the population to which generalisation is being made does not yet exist, there will be no aggregate statistics or other studies relating to it to which the authors can appeal. In these circumstances all we can do is to assess the plausibility of the authors' arguments about likely trends. Of course, if (as in the case of Cicourel and Kitsuse's study) we are reading a research report many years after the research was completed, we might be able to assess the plausibility of generalisation of the study's findings ourselves by drawing on more recent statistics or subsequent studies in the same field. And this is a strategy that may be available to us wherever authors cannot or do not make use of these resources themselves.

There is no doubt that ethnographic studies can, and probably already do, provide descriptive information about settings that are typical in relevant respects of larger aggregates that are of interest to us. However, in general, ethnographers are not very effective in establishing the typicality of what they report. And in the absence of such information we must often suspend judgement about the generalisability of their claims.[19]

CONCLUSION

In this chapter we have looked at assessing the validity of the major claims, the evidence for them, and the conclusions presented in ethnographic accounts. The starting point for such assessments is the face plausibility of the claims in terms of the reader's background knowledge. I argued in Chapter 3 that the level of plausibility required by researchers should be higher, on average, than that demanded by others. However, there will be many (usually evidential rather than major) claims that can be reasonably judged to be sufficiently plausible as they stand to be acceptable. A second test is of credibility: the reader must judge the likelihood of error, given the danger of reactivity, the nature of the feature about which claims are being made, the circumstances in which the research was carried out, and what is known about the researcher. Where the claim is judged to be neither sufficiently plausible nor credible, any evidence offered in support of it must be considered, and if none is available then the validity of the claim should be judged uncertain. In assessing the evidence offered we must take account of the type of claim involved, since different types of claim require different kinds of evidence. All claims involve descriptions and here we must assess both the validity of the evidence itself and the strength of the inference from evidence to claim. Also, any generalisations within the case must be examined. In assessing evidence for explanations and predictions, over and above the assessment of their descriptive components, we must consider whether the theoretical assumptions involved are plausible and whether the explanatory factor appealed to is the most convincing one in the case concerned. With evaluations and prescriptions, again we must assess the descriptive claims involved but also look at the values on which they are based, their justification and application. Finally, I looked at the assessment of the conclusions drawn from the findings of ethnographic studies. I considered the sorts of evidence necessary to sustain theoretical inference and empirical generalisation.

As I indicated in Chapter 3, validity is only one aspect of the assessment of ethnographic research, relevance is equally important. I shall discuss this in the next chapter.

NOTES

1. It would be very surprising if we found that all the major claims of a study were sufficiently plausible to accept them at face value. After all, the result would be that the findings had little relevance, since they would tell us nothing that we did not already know. What this implies is that there is a trade-off between plausibility and relevance.

2. I shall deal with these various sources of error in more detail

when I discuss the assessment of evidence.

3. Examples of this usage are to be found in Hargreaves (1967) and Fuller (1980).

4. See Arnold (1970) for a collection of articles exemplifying and discussing the use of the concept of 'subculture'. The articles in Burgess (1986) provide useful discussions of other problematic sociological concepts.

5. Hammersley (1987b). Scarth (1987) also identifies some problems in allocating instances to Woods' types of survival strategy.

6. I am using the distinction between observers' reports and informants' accounts in a way that does not conform exactly to the more conventional distinction between observation and interviewing. In my view the latter does not capture accurately what is the most relevant methodological distinction: between the treatment of data as indicating something about the people, activities or settings observed (as observers' reports), and the use of data as a source of information about other people, activities or settings to which the data refer (as informants' accounts). As should become clear, these two uses of data involve different, though overlapping, sets of validity threat.

   Much of the time this distinction corresponds to the more conventional one, but there are exceptions. For example, Parker *et al.* report that 'magistrates themselves expounded the criminal families thesis to us' (p. 91) in interviews. In my terms this is an observer's report since the fact that the magistrates expounded this thesis is being used to tell us something about *them*, not about the families referred to. Indeed the researchers believe the magistrates to be mistaken in their views about 'criminal families'. Conversely, an ethnographer may treat some of what he or she hears in the course of participant observation as informants' accounts. Thus, in my study of an inner city school I used what the teachers said to one another in the staffroom as a source of information not just about their attitudes but also about their behaviour in classrooms on occasions that I had not been able to observe.

7. The authors refer to 'transcription' of official proceedings. This term is ambiguous, but it seems unlikely that they used audio-recording.

8. For a useful discussion of assessing the validity of documents, see Scott 1990: Ch. 2.

9. I have, of course, examined this evidence in abstraction from the rest of Pollert's data and argument, and that gives further support to her analysis.

10. The authors say that because the magistrate said this we 'might wonder' if the status of the car influenced the decision. But they seem to give some weight to this interpretation.

11. '"Due process" is a term meaning the conduct of legal proceedings according to established principles and rules which safeguard the position of the individual charged' (Walker, 1980).
12. I shall concentrate on Countyside here, though the claim relates to City as well.
13. Cressey did investigate some cases where the conditions of his theory held, but not in a systematic way. For fuller discussion of these issues, see Hammersley (1989a).
14. What I shall present here is a rational reconstruction of these studies: my discussion will not match perfectly or exhaust the purposes of their authors. For a more extended account of this research, see Hammersley (1985).
15. Lacey is, of course, aware of these factors and incorporates them into his account, but as subordinate factors to differentiation. Also, the evidence that he provides about the effects of differentiation within the classroom adds further support to his case that differentiation was the main factor.
16. One thing that did not remain the same was the pupils, and differences between the cohorts of pupils may have affected Ball's findings. Also, the change in organisational structure itself may have had a temporary effect on attitudes.
17. There has been some additional work on this theory: see, for example, Quine (1974), Lacey (1974) and Abraham (1989).
18. The belief that statistical sampling theory is the only reasonable basis for empirical generalisation is another example of the misguided search for certainty that I criticised in Chapter 3. It is sometimes assumed that statistical techniques can provide the basis for knowing with certainly whether findings are generalisable. They cannot do this. Even at best, they only tell us what are the chances of the generalisation being false.
19. As I noted in Chapter 2, ethnographers rarely distinguish between theoretical inference and empirical generalisation in a very clear way. As a result, the arguments they put forward often combine the two. In such circumstances, we must consider the validity of the conclusions both as theoretical inferences and as empirical generalisations.

CHAPTER 5

Making an assessment: relevance

I argued in Chapter 3 that it was not sufficient for the findings of an ethnographic study to be true for them to have value. Equally important is that they make a contribution to knowledge that is relevant to some public concern. In this chapter I want to discuss the nature of relevance in more detail, and to look at some of the problems and controversies involved in assessing studies in terms of this criterion.

It seems to me that there are two aspects of relevance:

1. *The importance of the topic.* The research topic must relate (however remotely) to an issue of public importance.
2. *The contribution of the conclusions to existing knowledge.* The research findings must add something to our knowledge of the issue to which they relate. Research that merely confirms what is already beyond reasonable doubt makes no contribution.

In these terms research findings may connect with an important topic but still not be relevant since they do not tell us anything new about it. For instance, research informing us that the police are sometimes involved in violent incidents would have little relevance, even though it concerns an important issue, because it tells us something we already know. Conversely, findings may be novel but of little relevance because they do not relate to any issue of significance. For example, the fact that in Amsterdam early one Friday afternoon in the 1970s a police van came to pick up an old man and two dogs (Punch, 1979: 138) is news to all of us in the sense that we did not know it before, but it has little general importance (as far as I know) and therefore little relevance (nor does Punch claim otherwise). Importance and contribution are necessary and jointly sufficient conditions for relevance, and we must assess any set of findings in terms of both.

IMPORTANCE

Assessment of the relevance of ethnographic studies, and especially of the importance of the research focus, is even more open to uncertainty and disagreement than assessments of their validity. I can illustrate this, and some of the problems involved, by looking at a debate that took place over an article about muggers by Robert Lejeune. He describes a typical mugging from the mugger's point of view, drawing on interviews with 45 people who had committed one or more muggings. He identifies the salient problems facing muggers in carrying out an attack (such as controlling their own fear and ensuring the 'cooperation' of the victim), along with the strategies used to deal with these problems (Lejeune, 1977). Judith Posner wrote a response to this article criticising its focus on several grounds (Posner, 1980). She was not challenging the validity of the claims made; indeed she comments that the study is 'painstaking and sensitive in its depiction' (p. 104). Rather, she argues that it amounts to a kind of 'bizarre sociological voyeurism' (p. 104).[1] And she suggests that this study reflects a trend in ethnographic studies in sociology away from work that is relevant to 'practical problems in the real world' towards studies that are 'detached and meaningless' (p. 109). She comments that 'the study of deviance has become an end in itself, a form of sociological entertainment' (p. 109).

Posner argues that the justification for social research lies in solving either practical or conceptual problems. In terms of the first sort of problem:

understanding the mugger's vulnerability should either help us to defend ourselves against him or to rehabilitate him after he is caught. (It could even help us catch him!)

However, she claims that 'Lejeune (. . .) never attends to such matters'. Furthermore, Lejeune's article does not address a conceptual problem either:

although he ends his article with brief allusions to vulnerability and ego, he never really ties in his research with an existing body of research on similar issues.

Posner suggests that the research is presented as 'a mere slice of life' which 'seems to exist for its own sake' (p. 110). And she concludes that:

Sociologists, especially sociologists in the deviance area, are probably frequently motivated to research the bizarre in much the same way that anthropologists have traditionally gotten a kick out of studying far and distant peoples. (p. 111)

Posner is here questioning the importance of Lejeune's research focus, claiming that he does not relate it to any important public issue. And she uses the discussion of his article to suggest that this is a general problem with ethnographic research, especially in the sociology of deviance.

This charge of voyeurism, an interest in the exotic for the personal (and perhaps deviant!) gratification of social scientists, has been made by others about the sociology of deviance (Liazos, 1972). And the criticism that research topics are chosen with little consideration for their public importance is sometimes directed at ethnographic research in other areas too. Posner herself refers to the study of 'conversational pausing' as a topic that might be thought of as trivial. And ethnomethodological research, which has included study of that topic, has often been the brunt of criticism for being concerned with trivia.[2] More conventional ethnographic research may also seem to be open to this charge. Take the following examples from one of the major journals publishing ethnographic research in sociology: 'the pet as a "family member"' (Hickrod and Schmitt, 1982), 'CB and the experience of sex typing' (Danneker and Kasen, 1981), 'amateur and professional astronomers' (Stebbins, 1982). Are these not trivial topics?

The question of the importance of research topics is certainly a key issue that both producers and readers of ethnographic work must consider. However, it requires careful consideration. In Chapter 3 I pointed to the pressure for relevance to be defined in narrow terms of immediate payoff for practical problems. I argued there that it was essential that researchers be allowed to investigate both issues that ought to be problematic for practitioners but are not, and topics whose relevance to public issues is indirect and perhaps quite remote (because a division of labour is necessary within research).[3] I also drew attention to how our sense of what topics are important can be shaped by assumptions that are a product of our everyday concerns and/or of the historically produced relevances built into particular social science disciplines. Sometimes these relevances are reasonable enough, but sometimes they are not.

The implication of these points is that one cannot always tell at a glance what the importance of a research topic is. It is easy to dismiss topics as trivial simply because one does not recognise the links that they have with more important issues; or because they do not relate to matters that are conventionally regarded as of significance. I can illustrate the first of these points by reference to one of the examples mentioned earlier. While *apparently* trivial, the study of pauses in conversation, along with work on other aspects of conversational organisation, has relevance both to studies of power relations in communication between women and men (Beattie, 1984) and to investigations of political oratory and its effects (Atkinson, 1984). And these are topics of some importance. Similarly that reliance on conventional views about what is important may be defective is illustrated by another topic referred to above: the study of 'pets as family members'. Loneliness is a major social problem in modern industrial societies, and the keeping of animal pets is a strategy used by many to cope with that problem. From this point of view, the study of pets could well be an important topic. Equally, people's attitudes towards and relationships with pets are of significance for the issue of animal rights. In some respects the pet is in a privileged situation compared to humans' treatment of other types of animal; but it may none the less be a situation that has unacceptable aspects (for example, the caging of birds, the castration of dogs and cats, etc.).[4] This is not to say that all of the topics that ethnographic research addresses are important, and we might well disagree about the examples I have discussed. The point is simply that we must reflect carefully on the importance of particular studies, rather than making snap judgements.

The case of Lejeune's study of muggers is more straightforward, I think, than the examples I have discussed above. It is not difficult to see mugging as an important public issue that ought to be addressed by research. And Lejeune's specific focus on the strategies used by muggers might well contribute to our ability to reduce the incidence of this crime, to apprehend and rehabilitate muggers; even though it does not do this directly.[5] Posner's dismissal of the importance of Lejeune's research seems to have arisen from the fact that he did not provide a rationale for it that she found convincing. This raises a particularly important issue about how we set about assessing relevance: how far we must rely on the rationales provided by authors themselves.

While the authors of ethnographic accounts usually do give some rationale for their research focus, this is not *always* the case. Here is the opening paragraph of French and French's article on 'Gender imbalances in the primary classroom':

It is now well established that in mixed sex classrooms male pupils receive more teacher attention than do females. Brophy and Good, for example, have observed that 'boys have more interactions with the teacher than girls and appear to be generally more salient in the teacher's perceptual field' (1970, p. 373). Stanworth (1981) and Spender (1982) have also noted an imbalance in this respect and, although their formulation is more tentative, Galton, Simon and Croll's conclusion is in essence the same: 'There does appear to be a slight tendency for . . . boys to receive more contact than girls' (1980, p. 66).

The present study reveals imbalances in teacher–pupil contact which, in broad terms, are compatible with these observations. However, rather than simply reporting the occurrence of the imbalances (. . .) (t)he principal aim of this study is to provide the basis for (. . .) an explanation(. . .). (French and French, 1984: 127)

There is a clear account here of the focus of the research, and of its relationship to other literature. However, there is no indication of why this focus is believed to be important; nor does one occur elsewhere in the article.

Whether justification for a research focus is necessary, and how much is required, are matters of judgement. There is no naturally given end point to the process of justification. However much is provided, we could in principle always ask for more. And it follows from this that some topics may be judged to need little or no justification. For example, Lejeune provides the following rationale for his account of the strategies adopted by muggers:

> In contrast to the public indignation and journalistic concern generated by this type of street crime (. . .), (mugging) suffers from neglect on the part of sociologists. (Lejeune, 1977: 123)

In my view, while this is extremely brief it is sufficient. The relationship of his research to the question of how mugging occurs and therefore to how it might be avoided and discouraged is obvious. By contrast, I do not find French and French's topic of such clear importance. (You may not agree, but I must ask you to share my doubts for a moment.) The appropriate response to a lack of what the reader believes to be sufficient justification is not to conclude (as Posner seems to do) that the study is without justification, but rather to consider whether a plausible rationale for the focus can be constructed. Here is my effort to do this for French and French's study. In this case there seem to be at least two, by no means incompatible, bases for justification:

1. that an imbalance in classroom participation, or teacher attention, between boys and girls is unfair in itself;
2. that this imbalance is believed to contribute significantly to differential school performance and occupational placement, and thus to differences of income, status and power between the sexes in adult life.

What is involved in constructing a rationale is to show how the research topic might contribute to our knowledge about one or more policy issues that are (and/or ought to be) of public concern. And in assessing rationales for research foci, two considerations must be borne in mind: whether the focus can be linked, however remotely, to a value we accept as not in need of further justification; and whether the links between the focus and that value are judged to be sound.

In the case of French and French's article, I find the first possible justification (that an imbalance in teacher attention is unfair in itself) unconvincing because I do not accept the value to which appeal is made. Why should we insist that boys and girls in a class receive equal amounts of aggregate teacher attention? Surely we would expect teachers to take account, to one degree or another, of the individual characteristics of pupils in dealing with them: of variations in their background knowledge and their interests, their abilities and disabilities, the opportunities they have and have not had, etc., as well as of what they do in the classroom? All of these considerations may affect the amount of attention the teacher gives them. Of course, some of these characteristics will be randomly distributed with respect to sex, so that over time and across different school classes they will not produce aggregate differences between girls and boys; though we cannot assume that they will balance one another within a single lesson, and all of French and French's data come from one lesson. However, some of them may be systematically related to sex. An obvious example is that on average boys may be more prone to classroom disruption than girls. If this is so, then it is reasonable to expect that teachers would give more attention (in the form of warnings and reprimands) to some proportion of the boys, both for their own good and for that of the rest of the class. Given this, it is not obvious to me that equal aggregate teacher attention between the sexes is a good thing, in a single lesson or even over a long period. Here, the suggested value in terms of which the research focus is judged important is not one that I think it is reasonable to accept.

The other possible justification for French and French's research focus (that the differential distribution of teacher attention might help produce underachievement by girls in school that has consequences for their life chances) is problematic in another way. I accept the value that is appealed to (equality of educational and occupational opportunity between the sexes). However, I have doubts about the causal link between differential teacher attention and girls' underachievement. Once again, these doubts stem in large part from the authors' focus on *amount* of teacher attention. It seems unlikely that this is strongly related to levels of educational achievement. Much more plausible would be the claim that differences in the frequency of particular *types* of teacher attention, such as praise and blame, might affect achievement levels. Here, then, I accept the importance of the value issue to which this rationale appeals, but I have doubts about the effective relevance of the study to that value.

We can see from my discussion of French and French's study that rationales for research foci always involve value assumptions, and often factual assumptions as well. And assessing the importance of a topic requires us to make judgements about those assumptions. I tried to show in Chapter 3 that while arguments about both facts and values cannot be resolved by simple demonstrations based on premises that are beyond all possible doubt, neither is outside the scope of rational argument. In both cases appeal must be made to grounds that the person advancing the argument accepts as beyond reasonable doubt and that the intended audience can reasonably be expected to accept in the same way. One of my criticisms of French and French's paper is that they assume that the justification for their focus is obvious and sound; whereas, in my view, it is neither. But, of course, in assessing the rationale for this study, I have taken the value of equal educational and occupational opportunites for men and women to be beyond doubt: not only do I accept it but I have assumed that you as reader do too, so that there is no need for me to provide justificatory argument in support of it. But I could be wrong about this. There are religious and political views which reject that value, arguing, for example, that women and men are suited to different spheres of life. The process of justification is potentially endless; and all we can do is to stop the argument where it seems reasonably unlikely that dispute will occur (and take it up again if we are proven wrong).

While I believe that Posner's assessment of Lejeune's study is largely misconceived because it ignores the justification for that study's focus – which can be constructed relatively easily and convincingly – I think her argument does raise an important issue about the *coordination* of ethnographic studies. Even where studies do explicitly relate their research focus to public issues, they rarely seem to be well coordinated with one another to deal with those issues. It is not enough for studies to be loosely related to matters of public concern, they should be collectively organised to address those matters. In my view this coordination is weak at best in many areas. This leads us into discussion of the other aspect of arguments about relevance: the question of the distinctive contribution that particular studies make.

CONTRIBUTION

Besides assessing whether the focus of a study is important we must also look at its relationship to other studies that are available, and to commonsense knowledge. Here the issue is what contribution the findings make to what we already know. As I noted earlier, a study's findings might be important but contribute little because they are already well established through research and/or merely confirm what we already take to be beyond reasonable doubt on the basis of everyday experience.[6]

An example of criticism of research for failing to make a contribution to our knowledge can be found in some comments on a recent study of market traders (Cherrington *et al.*, 1987). Pinch and Clark's article focuses on 'patter merchants', traders who engage in an elaborate 'spiel' which attracts an audience and persuades some of its members to buy the goods on offer. The authors examine the structure of such 'spiels', using conversational analysis to show how their structure is designed to achieve mass sales: for example, through the use of contrasts that highlight the supposed value and low price of what is on offer (Pinch and Clark, 1986). Cherrington *et al.* accept that the operation of local markets is an important sociological topic, but they deny that Pinch and Clark tell us anything new about this topic:

Our impression is that, crucially, much of the analysis consists of a description of the sales pitch which is rather obvious to most people who have ever bought goods in an English market. (. . .) That market pitchers use talk and non-verbal communication to try to persuade people to buy goods which they might not actually want, and have a measure of success in doing this, should come as no great revelation to anyone. Whilst this lack of anything other than 'common-sense' description struck us most forcibly, Pinch and Clark clearly believe that they are describing something which we could not have known without their research, and that the results are important, even revelatory. We can only conclude that the authors' naive fascination with the 'accomplishment' of the pitchers' talk led them to minimise the importance of the social interaction, to the detriment of the seriousness and relevance of their sociology. (Cherrington *et al.*, 1987: 278 and 279)[7]

In making an assessment of criticisms such as these, we must consider the various ways in which studies may contribute to existing knowledge. It is perhaps worth emphasising, first, that the test of 'contribution' does not rule out the value of all studies that confirm previous findings. I argued in Chapter 3 that within the research community the level of routine scepticism about what is known should be higher than outside, that it should be determined by the common ground among researchers of different political views, practical interests and experience. Given this, there is considerable scope for research designed to check the findings of previous studies, especially where this involves triangulation: the use of sources of information likely to involve different types and directions of validity threat compared to the original study. Indeed, one sort of contribution that research can make is to test previous findings and put them beyond reasonable doubt.

Perhaps the most common contribution claimed for ethnographic studies is that they fill a gap in the literature, in the sense of dealing with a phenomenon about which there has been little previous research. As we saw, this was the rationale that Lejeune provided for his study of mugging, and Pinch and Clark adopt the same justification. They open their article by claiming that 'There is no body of research which has systematically examined the interactional skills and processes involved in selling (. . .)' (Pinch and Clark, 1986: 169).

The principle behind this sort of rationale is developed by Howard Becker in his discussion of the Chicago School studies of the 1920s and 1930s. He argues that these formed part of a mosaic that provided a picture of Chicago social life as it was at that time (Becker, 1966). While subsequent studies have not been so geographically specific, the same sort of rationale applies in the sense that they may give us a picture of the various categories of actor and situation making up modern societies. Thus, we have studies telling us about the perspectives and practices of police officers and tramps, prostitutes and doctors, journalists and drug dealers, etc., and of the settings and institutions in which they are involved.

It should be noted, however, that this rationale involves a problematic element of empirical generalisation. There is heterogeneity as well as homogeneity among such categories of actor and institution.[8] And this indicates another important way in which ethnographic studies may complement one another. Studies may contribute to the literature by providing information about other cases in a population that previous studies have sought to generalise about on the basis of too small or homogeneous a sample. As we saw in Chapter 4, ethnographic studies frequently claim that the cases they studied are typical, so that generalisation to some larger population can be made, but that often this is not justified. And we noted there how other studies, especially of cases strategically selected to contrast with those investigated previously, would allow much more convincing generalisation and also document the sorts of heterogeneity to be found within the population. You may remember that it was in these terms that Punch justified his study of policing in the Warmoesstraat district of Amsterdam: that there had been a relative neglect of policing in the inner city by researchers and that his study would thereby extend the empirical basis for generalisations about police work (Punch, 1979).

Such plugging of gaps in our current knowledge, whether in the form of studies in previously neglected areas or of research that widens the basis for sound generalisation, is not the only way in which the findings of ethnographic accounts can make an important contribution. They may also serve to challenge and reformulate what were previously taken to be facts, whether on the basis of everyday experience or of previous studies. A striking example is to be found in research on 'soccer hooliganism' where findings are often contrasted with defective commonsense and media understandings of the phenomenon. Peter Marsh, for example, tries to show that, contrary to the widespread assumption that the behaviour of football fans is disorderly, it is ritually structured and highly predictable; and therefore less dangerous for participants and bystanders than might appear (Marsh *et al* 1978). Dunning *et al.* (1988), dealing with the same topic, argue that contrary to popular belief hooliganism has accompanied association football ever since its establishment in the 1870s and 1880s, and that it is not a fashion that will lapse in due course but a way of life for those engaged in it (Dunning *et al.*, 1988). Clearly, such revision of what was previously accepted as knowledge can be of great value (assuming, of course, that the new knowledge is itself valid).

Equally, studies may be concerned with checking whether previously established facts are still true. Here the interest is in the extent and character of social change. The most obvious illustrations of this are community restudies. For example the primary motivation of the Lynds in restudying Middletown was to discover how life there had changed as a result of the Depression (Lynd and Lynd, 1937). Similarly, in studying Plainville the Gallahers took the information provided by West's original study as a base-line from which to chart the changes that had occurred in the town during the intervening fifteen years (Gallaher, 1964). The same sort of motivation sometimes underlies studies of different cases of the same *category* of phenomena at different times. Thus, Ball was concerned with whether the same processes of differentiation and polarisation discovered under the selective education system by Hargreaves and Lacey would also be found in schools after comprehensive reform in English education (Hargreaves, 1967; Lacey, 1970; Ball, 1981).

Finally, studies may be related to one another in that they contribute to the development and testing of the same theory. The studies by Hargreaves, Lacey and Ball make a contribution in this way too (a fact which illustrates that accounts may make more than one type of contribution to our knowledge). As we saw in the previous chapter, these studies develop and test differentiation-polarisation theory in settings that both vary the level of differentiation and control some of the other relevant variables. In this way they complement one another in a manner that few other ethnographic studies have achieved (Hammersley, 1985).

It is in terms of these sorts of relationship between the findings of a study and existing knowledge that we need to assess the contribution made by those findings. Studies are not always explicit about the contribution they are intended to make, and are often not directed towards other literature in such a way that they produce a cumulation of knowledge in any very clear and effective manner. There is a strong tendency for ethnographic accounts to be produced so as, in large part, to stand alone, having only weak relationships to other studies. This is encouraged by the conceptualisation of their goal in terms of theoretical description, whereby great emphasis is placed on the particular case studied. Much as many anthropologists conceive of themselves as producing knowledge about their chosen tribe, so ethnographic sociologists often seem to view themselves as simply describing a setting for its own sake. While they recognise that general conclusions must be drawn, the relationship between these and those of other studies is often not very strong. Another factor is an excessive emphasis on novelty. A result of this is that much more ethnographic research is concerned with opening up new areas or generating new analytical approaches than is devoted to systematically building on what has been done before. In my view we need to move to a situation where there is less emphasis on the investigation of new phenomena or the generation of new ideas (important as these are) and more on improving existing knowledge, whether empirical, theoretical, or methodological. This will require that the links among studies be made more explicit and stronger, so that the contribution of past research and the priorities for future research become clearer.

CONCLUSION

In this chapter I have looked at two components of relevance: the importance of the topic and the contribution of the findings. And I have discussed some of the difficulties and disagreements involved in their application to the assessment of ethnographic studies. As with the assessment of validity, the assessment of the relevance of a study is a matter of judgement; and, even more obviously than in the case of validity, it can lead to disagreement. There is no simple answer or easy route to consensus. But that does not mean that we cannot make rational judgements about the relevance of ethnographic research; or that we should not seek consensus. In the next chapter I shall present a detailed discussion of one of my own articles to provide a more extended illustration of what is involved in assessing the validity and relevance of an ethnographic account.

NOTES

1. She also questions its ethicality: whether its publication was likely to have unacceptable consequences. I shall discuss this issue in Chapter 7. There are several published replies to Posner: Lejeune (1980); Sagarin (1980); and Cohen (1980).
2. See McNall and Johnson (1975) for an example. For an ethnomethodological reply to this criticism, see Sharrock and Anderson (1986).
3. I take Posner's distinction between practical and conceptual problems to refer to the need for such a division of labour.
4. Interestingly, while the article referred to here touches on both these issues, neither is its main focus: it uses the family pet as a case for developing and testing Goffman's frame analysis (Hickrod and Schmitt, 1982).
5. Lejeune had also studied victims of mugging. His interest in the topic was stimulated by being mugged himself.
6. As I noted in the previous chapter, there is a trade-off between plausibility and contribution. The more plausible are findings, the less of a contribution they will make; and the more of a contribution they make, the less likely they can be accepted as plausible at face value.
7. For Pinch and Clark's reply to these charges. see Pinch and Clark (1987).
8. This problem arises with the Chicago studies too. Becker notes that Chicagoans tended to view Chicago as typical of other cities, though they rarely addressed this issue explicitly.

CHAPTER 6

An example

In previous chapters I have outlined and illustrated the principles which I believe ought to guide the reading and assessment of ethnographic studies. In this chapter I provide an example of a sustained assessment of an ethnographic article and thereby, in what I hope is the most useful way, exemplify the application of the principles I have advocated.

The article I shall assess is reprinted in Appendix 1. It is an account of the functions of the talk among teachers found in a secondary school staffroom. I wrote it some years ago on the basis of ethnographic fieldwork, carried out in the early 1970s, in a school I called 'Downtown'. Assessing one's own research is as important as assessing anyone else's. However, in doing so one is in both a more and a less privileged position than other readers: one knows more of the background, but is perhaps not able to attain the same critical distance. You will have to judge how far (and how legitimately) I have made use of the advantage and how well I have overcome the disadvantage. Indeed, you might wish to carry out your own assessment of the article and compare it with mine.

I shall begin by providing a summary of the article, using the framework suggested in Chapter 2. Then I shall assess the validity of the claims made and the relevance of the research focus and the conclusions drawn.

SUMMARY

The general focus of this study is social interaction among teachers in school staffrooms, and the information we can gain from it about the structure of social relationships among teachers. However, the more specific topic is the exchange of 'news' about pupils among teachers, the aim being to describe and explain the features of this news exchange. Only a very brief rationale is presented: appealing to previous neglect of the general focus, and its significance for the sociology of occupations and for explaining teachers' behaviour in classrooms.

The case studied is the staffroom in a 'small, inner-city, boys' secondary modern school'. No further information about the school is provided in this article, though more can be found in a research biography published elsewhere, and in the PhD thesis from which the article derives (Hammersley, 1984; Hammersley, 1980). The thesis tells us much about the school's local context, internal organisation and history. It was located within an inner-city area of a large northern conurbation which was occupied by many Asian and 'West Indian' families, as well as by some white 'problem' families. In the past the building had been an elementary school, but after it became a secondary modern in the early 1950s it was one of the few such schools to have a GCE stream. As a result, it had attracted pupils from outside its catchment area. In more recent years, however, this inflow of pupils had stopped as a result of the opening of a new school nearby. The number of pupils had dropped as a result to around 300, half of what it had been; and pupils were no longer entered for GCE. Many of the teachers at the school had taught there for several years, witnessing what they regarded as a sharp decline in the quality of the pupils.

No information is given about methods in the article, though we can assume participant observation in the staffroom was involved (in what role is not clear). Again, further information is available in the other sources. Most of the data were gathered by the researcher sitting in the staffroom and participating in or overhearing conversations among the teachers. Some also arose from conversations between teachers and the researcher on the way to or from classrooms or staffroom (and in the strict sense was therefore not staffroom talk). The fieldwork took place over a period of two terms, the researcher spending three days a week in the school, on average. The researcher was much younger than most of the teachers, and was regarded as inexperienced by them; being treated in many respects like the students on teaching practice who were present in the school for much of the fieldwork period. The data were fieldnotes based on jotted notes made on the spot and written up in the evenings. The researcher was not a teacher in the school, and his role as researcher was overt. However, the teachers did not know that he was taking notes about what they said in the staffroom.

The major claims made in the article consist of both description and explanation of the staffroom talk. There are three main descriptive claims. First, there is the identification of four types of staffroom news, dealing with:

1. specific events
2. the moods of particular classes
3. the presence or absence of 'trouble-makers'
4. summary typifications of troublesome pupils.

These are supported by extracts from fieldnotes instancing each type.

Second, there is the claim that staffroom news is preoccupied with threats to classroom order. The fieldnote extracts illustrating the types of news are intended to support this claim too. There is also an examination of exceptions to this generalisation: news items dealing with the pupils' ability.

Third, it is claimed that underlying staffroom talk at Downtown there is a standard set of pupil types, consisting of: the 'unstable', the 'louts', the 'easily led', and the 'immature'. It is also noted that the teachers recognised that pupils sometimes moved between these types over time. Each of these pupil typifications is illustrated with fieldnote extracts, as are teachers' discussions of changes in the character of individual pupils.

There seem to be two main explanatory claims:

1. Staffroom news is exchanged at Downtown because it provides information that teachers find useful given their work circumstances: they work in separate classrooms but recurrently face the same pupils. Little or no evidence is provided for this over and above that presented in support of the descriptive claims.

2. Staffroom news is not just a matter of information exchange but is also 'rhetorical'. It involves accounting for pupils' indiscipline in such a way as to deflect blame for it away from the teachers and from the approach to teaching to which they are committed. Additional fieldnote extracts recording staffroom talk are provided and analysed to show that their structure is compatible with this interpretation; and two published sources are also drawn upon.

There are no conclusions in the article that explicitly go beyond the case. However, these must be implied given the nature of the stated research focus. I think we must assume that the author intended the main claims about Downtown either to provide the basis for empirical generalisation to other staffrooms (though no population is specified) or to relate to some theoretical inference about the functions of staffroom talk. It is difficult to be more specific than this (even for me!).

VALIDITY

Definitions

There are a couple of minor definitional issues. First, there is the use of the (much-abused) term 'rhetorical'. Strictly speaking, 'rhetoric' refers simply to the stylistic strategies used in oral (and perhaps also written) presentations. There is a derogatory usage, indicating something that is persuasively presented but unsound; and something like this is presumably intended here. The implication is that the function of staffroom talk is not merely referential (as it needs to be for exchanging information). Rather, it is designed to reinforce certain already held assumptions on the part of the speaker (and others) and thereby to provide reassurance. It might be clearer to refer to this as the reassurance or reinforcement (rather than the rhetorical) function of staffroom talk.

The other issue concerns the 'cutting out' of context. All descriptions cut out some parts of the context of the events described, and include others. What is argued here, in effect, is that contextual features which the author regards as important for explaining pupils' behaviour are omitted from staffroom talk at Downtown. While the author's judgement about this matter may be reasonable, it is important to recognise that what is highlighted is the cutting out of (some aspects of) *social* context rather than the cutting out of context *per se*.

Descriptive claims

I do not believe that we can accept any of these claims at face value as sufficiently plausible; and their credibility probably does require support with evidence, which the author provides. There are a number of questions that we must ask about this evidence, however. First, we need to consider the possible effects of reactivity. While data collection in the staffroom was covert, the researcher's identity as researcher was known, and so we cannot rule out procedural reactivity. Personal reactivity is clearly also a possibility. The fact that the researcher seems to have been regarded as low status by the teachers, however, suggests that reactivity may not have led them to hide their views and actions. And the data themselves suggest that much which might have been hidden was not. The fact that the researcher was in the field for a lengthy and fairly intensive period of time would also reduce the danger of the teachers maintaining a front for the researcher, since fronts are difficult to sustain over long periods. On balance, the risk that reactivity has seriously distorted the data seems low.[1]

Second, we must ask how accurately what the teachers said was recorded? Since the data were fieldnotes, not transcriptions of audio-recordings, this perhaps indicates some inaccuracy. And the fact that observation in the staffroom was covert added to the problem, as the author indicates in the research biography:

Noting down what was said on the spot was very difficult, being done in a surreptitious and hurried manner. On one occasion I was forced to jot down notes on the newspaper I was reading, hoping that no-one would ask to borrow it. There had been comments on one occasion about me reading a 'liberal' newspaper like *The Guardian* and on that basis I hoped I was safe! Often jotted notes had to be made after I had left the staffroom. While I tried to note down literally what was said, I may have made mistakes. While I can claim that even where I did not get the words exactly right I probably got the sense of what was said, that unfortunately builds in a reliance on the interpretation of sense I made on the spot. Also important here is the relevance of context. I often wonder now in reading these data whether anything was said before or after the recorded exchange which would modify interpretation of it. Once again there is reliance here on my on-the-spot decisions. Even more important, it is possible that on some occasions, rather than simply not remembering the exact words used, I may have forgotten whole sentences or stretches of conversation which came between one utterance and the next in the recorded exchange. (Hammersley, 1984: 53–4)

Obviously, this does raise a serious threat to validity. What is especially important to consider is whether any systematic bias seems likely to have been operating (perhaps unconsciously) on the researcher's data recording. For example, his political views about the authoritarian character of traditional teaching (which are revealed in the research biography) may have led him to misinterpret and/or select comments in such a way that they confirmed his expectations. What is at issue here is the relationship between what was recorded in the fieldnotes and what actually occurred in the Downtown staffroom during the period of the fieldwork. Selective bias may have been operating on the part of the researcher, and we have no basis for checking this. On balance, though, it seems unlikely that the validity of the account would be wholly undermined by this problem.

Another issue concerns generalisability within the case: how far is the staffroom talk of the whole staff during the relevant period captured accurately? Thirteen teachers are quoted in the article, out of a total of nineteen; but some much more frequently than others. In his research biography the author notes that he had much closer contact with some teachers than with others. Might his account of staffroom culture at Downtown have been biased by this differential contact? In my judgement, this seems relatively unlikely, given the degree of coverage of the staff and the fact that many of the comments recorded were made in public, often involving collaboration between multiple speakers, and apparently without any signs of disagreement. Similarly, while we are not told from what stage of the fieldwork the various quotes come, there seems no obvious reason to suppose that they are likely to be unrepresentative of the whole.[2]

However, while this may be true in general terms, we may still raise questions about the representativeness of the data used to support particular claims. For example, was it really the case that the teachers used a standard set of four pupil types? Even on the basis of the data supplied, it seems unlikely that there was stability, either over time or across all the teachers. Certainly, the *terms* used to refer to the pupils in the extracts quoted in the article are much more diverse than this, and include at least one that does not match the typology, namely 'good lads' (Extract 14).

Finally, we must consider the relationship between the data extracts and the claims they are intended to support. In my judgement this relationship is generally strong; there are no obvious contrary interpretations.

Explanatory claims

Of course the validity of the explanatory claims depends, in part, on that of the descriptive claims discussed above. For the purposes of the assessment here I shall assume that the descriptions are for the most part valid.

The first explanatory claim seems plausible. There is little description of the circumstances in which these teachers work in the article, but the claim that they work in separate classrooms and teach many of the same pupils can be accepted as plausible and credible at face value, I believe. Furthermore, the character of the news exchanged is compatible with this explanation. And the implicit theoretical idea (that in such circumstances teachers will seek and be influenced by information about particular pupils drawn from colleagues) seems reasonable; and there are no *more* plausible alternative explanations for the character of the staffroom talk obvious to me.

The second explanatory claim, by contrast, *is* problematic. While reading off the motivation of staffroom comments from their content seems reasonably convincing in the case of the first claim, here it is less so. The author provides evidence to try to establish that the nature of staffroom talk is compatible with the idea that it serves a reassurance or reinforcement, as well as an information exchange, function. Crucial here is the way that the accounts of pupils' behaviour exchanged by the teachers cut out the social context surrounding that behaviour, and especially the teachers' own actions. And, indeed, it does seem that all the extracts quoted in the article have this feature.[3] Of course, we do not know whether those quoted are representative of the corpus of data collected, though we can check this against the complete set of data presented in the thesis (and we find, I think, that they are representative in this respect). More difficult to assess is whether these data are representative of staffroom news exchanged at Downtown in the relevant period. There is no way of checking this, but I think we can take the data quoted as indicating a tendency for staffroom news at Downtown to have this character.

There is little description of the explanatory factor itself: the teachers' need for reassurance. It is simply claimed that the Downtown teachers find the failure of the pupils to live up to their expectations threatening. However, I think we can accept this as sufficiently plausible at face value, and there is some evidence in the thesis to support it.

The theoretical assumption involved in this explanation (that, faced with failure teachers committed to a traditional conception of teaching will blame either themselves or the pupils (and/or parents)), also seems plausible. There is, however, at least one other reasonable explanation for the way in which staffroom news excluded the social context of the event described: that the teachers simply believed (perhaps rightly) that psychological factors were the most important ones causing pupils' behaviour. The author does not address this issue; he avoids it in large part by the sleight of hand involved in using 'cutting out context' to refer to cutting out social context. He trades on the fact that no one could reasonably deny the relevance of context to explanations. Explanations necessarily appeal to some contextual feature as the causal factor. The relevance of *social* context, on the other hand, needs to be argued for, but no such argument is provided.[4] The implicit argument that the author adopts is that, since the staff's explanations do not properly explain, they must be excuses. But given that the premiss of this argument has not been established, we should not accept the conclusion. And on top of this, the logic of the argument itself is questionable. There is no reason to assume that because an explanation is false its communication must have been intended to serve some other function than that of providing true information (any more than we should assume that the communication of a true explanation cannot be intended to serve some other function than information exchange). All this is not to reject the explanation offered, simply to point out that there are some serious problems in establishing it which are not addressed in this article or in the other sources.

Conclusions

As I noted earlier, no conclusions are presented in the article. The discussion under the heading of 'Conclusion' simply summarises the main claims. However, given the declared focus of the research, we must assume that some broader conclusions are implied. And since it is not made clear whether what is intended is theoretical inference or empirical generalisation, we must consider the possibility of each. It should be said, though, that neither looks promising.

If what is intended is empirical generalisation, we must ask: to what population is it believed that the findings should be generalisable? The focus seems to relate to all schools. Yet, even putting aside the illegitimacy of such unrestricted generalisation, it seems most unlikely that many of the features of this school would be generalisable even to other secondary schools in England and Wales in the 1970s. The fact that it was a secondary modern, that it was single sex, and its small size were all atypical features even in the 1970s; and these probably have consequences which make the case atypical in other respects too. It may be that the school is typical of small, boys' inner-city secondary moderns in the early 1970s, but the author does not tell us why we should be interested in this population, nor is there any obvious reason for us to be interested. Furthermore, there is insufficient evidence even for this generalisation to be established.

Justifying inference from case to focus on the basis of theoretical inference is perhaps more promising. There are theoretical ideas in the account, notably concerning the functions of staffroom talk. However, these seem to be used as a basis for explaining the features found in the Downtown staffroom, rather than being put forward as theoretical ideas that have been tested in this case. For the latter to be convincing, we would need to be told why the case of Downtown is especially appropriate for a test of these ideas. No such rationale is provided. One might argue that Downtown was a situation in which teachers were subjected to maximum threat to their identities as competent practitioners (and something like this is hinted at in the thesis); but we need more clarification of the theory and of the relationship of the case to it before we can come to any reasonable judgement about the soundness of the theoretical inference involved.

RELEVANCE

If the conclusions of this article were to be interpreted as limited to Downtown school itself, the relevance of the study would be very low. Few people would be interested in what happened in a single, pseudonymous school in the early 1970s (especially one which closed down soon after the research was completed). On this basis, while the research could be deemed to make a contribution (in the limited sense in which I have used the term in this book), the information it provides must be judged of little or no importance.

If wider conclusions are assumed, we must consider what their relevance might be. Here the brief rationale provided serves some purpose. It is fairly clear, I think, that what teachers say in the staffroom may tell us a good deal about staff relationships, and that the nature of those relationships is of considerable importance for many aspects of schooling, including the nature and effects of teachers' typifications of pupils. Furthermore, it is true that there has been little or no other research in this area, so that research of this kind would make a useful contribution (though as I made clear in Chapter 5, in my view this is the weakest form of contribution). Unfortunately, though, the value of these general conclusions is largely undermined by their questionable validity.

CONCLUSION

In summary, then, most of the descriptive claims and the first of the explanatory claims are established reasonably convincingly: the Downtown teachers do seem to have engaged in the exchange of news (of the four types specified) concerned primarily with threats to classroom order; and this does seem likely to have arisen from the character of their working conditions, that they worked separately but faced many of the same pupils. The other, and much more important, explanatory claim (that news exchange also served the purpose of reinforcing the teachers' existing assumptions about the pupils and about teaching) is less well-established. While the data seem to fit it, and the theoretical assumption on which it is based is reasonable, there are problems with the author's attempt to establish the priority of this explanation. This is because he relies on drawing conclusions about the function of staffroom comments from the judgement (itself unsubstantiated) that the explanations which they contain are inadequate. An even more serious problem with this article is that it provides no basis for drawing more general conclusions from the evidence about this case, and no sound basis seems available. And, while restricting the conclusions to the claims made about Downtown would avoid this problem, it would give the findings little or no relevance.

All this does not imply that the article is completely valueless. Its focus is of fairly clear relevance, and it may offer useful comparative data and theoretical ideas for subsequent studies. However, I think that we must conclude that its value is rather limited.

In this chapter I have looked at how the approach I outlined in earlier chapters might be applied to the assessment of a whole article. In the final chapter I shall look at how this sort of assessment relates to some other concerns we may have in reading ethnographic studies.

NOTES

1. We should be a little careful here, however. Punch (1979: 13) reports that he only discovered by chance, at a party long after the fieldwork, how much the police officers he studied had hidden from him; despite giving him much self-incriminating data.

2. There is a brief discussion of this issue in the research biography (Hammersley, 1984: 52–3). Also, the thesis includes all the data that were recorded in the staffroom during the fieldwork, and the date of collection of each data item is indicated.

3. Extract 1 may seem to be an exception, but it is not. Information about the incident to which Greaves was responding is elicited by 'What had he (the pupil) done?', and his reply concentrates entirely on the character of the pupil.

4. Ironically, I refer to this point in Note 9 in criticising others; but proceed to make the same mistake myself.

CHAPTER 7

Conclusion: varieties of assessment

As I noted at the beginning of this book, the reading of ethnographic accounts has been given much less attention than it deserves. More significantly, the issue of the criteria by which such accounts should be assessed raises fundamental issues about the nature of ethnography on which there is little consensus. The approach I have taken is not, therefore, one that all ethnographers would accept. I have sought to steer a path between, on the one hand, those views of ethnographic methodology that are based on a naive realism whereby the goal is simply to represent social phenomena 'in their own terms', and on the other hand those that abandon realism in favour of an emphasis on direct practical payoff and/or the creativity of ethnographic analysis and writing. In doing so I advocated what I called a 'subtle realism' in which the goal is still to represent reality, but in a way that is relevant to particular purposes or values; and with a recognition that even claims about validity, and especially those about relevance, can only be judged on the basis of assumptions whose own validity we can never know for certain. At the same time, I have argued for the distinctive character and role of the research community, both in adopting a higher level of routine scepticism and a stronger commitment to resolving disagreement by debate than is found elsewhere, and in operating a division of labour that enables us to achieve knowledge that would not otherwise be available. Much of the book has been concerned with spelling out and illustrating the implications of this point of view for our reading of ethnographic texts.

The sort of assessment that I have been concerned with, while very important, is not the only kind. My primary concern has been with how, as researchers and students, we should read ethnographic accounts with a view to deciding whether they make a valuable contribution to our knowledge. While this probably shares much with other sorts of assessment, it does not exhaust the relevant issues. In this final chapter I shall consider briefly some other sorts of assessment: that carried out by practitioners[1]; that concerned with the competence of the researcher; and that dealing with the effectiveness and/or ethics of particular research strategies.

PRACTICAL ASSESSMENT

One sort of assessment that is obviously important, given my argument that research must have some ultimate relevance for other forms of practice, is practitioners' assessment of the value of research findings. It is worth distinguishing here between two sorts of use that practitioners may make of research (there are no doubt others): first, it may be employed to satisfy a need for information that is important to their work; second, it may be used to convince others of something in order to persuade them to adopt a particular, desirable policy.

In the first situation practitioners are likely to use the same two criteria of assessment that I outlined in earlier chapters. However, their interpretation of what is valid and relevant is likely to differ from that of researchers. It is sometimes suggested that for practical purposes we require a lower level of likely validity than is usually demanded by researchers. But while I have argued that researchers should operate at a higher level of routine doubt than others, this does not mean that in all circumstances the validity requirements of practitioners will be lower than those of researchers. Indeed, in some circumstances they may be higher. Practitioners' judgements will vary from those of researchers because their experience, and thus what they find plausible, differs. Also, the threshold of validity applied may well depend on what are taken to be the implications of the claims involved, and how significant these implications are judged to be. For example, where the information implies no change of current practice, the threshold in terms of which information is judged valid may be relatively low. But where the information implies radical action the threshold applied may be much higher. And in many circumstances this will be a reasonable approach. Furthermore, we must remember that different types of practitioner are likely to vary considerably in judgements about the validity of particular claims, because of the varying salience of that claim for their concerns and because of differing experience and background assumptions.

Variation between researchers and practitioners, and among practitioner groups, occurs even more obviously in relation to the criterion of relevance. Practitioners are likely to place great value on information that is directly relevant to the problems, chronic and acute, that they face. Ideally, what they want is information that goes a long way towards solving those problems and which is available in a user-friendly form at the time when it is needed. By contrast, for the most part, they are likely to be less interested in, and less likely to see the value of, information that relates only remotely, if at all, to those problems; especially if it is information that in their terms is already well known.

The other sort of value that research can have for practitioners is as a rhetorical resource in arguing the case for particular policies. Here the authority of research is used, and sometimes abused, for instrumental purposes. In this case, research findings are likely to be judged in terms of whether they support what the individual or group is seeking to promote, and whether they are likely to be convincing to the target audience.

This too is a legitimate role for research to play, it seems to me; even though it carries the danger that findings may be misinterpreted, presented as better established than they are, or judged wanting against standards that none could meet. It highlights the advantage that research gains from the higher threshold of scepticism it adopts, since it is precisely this which gives it the authority to be used in this way. What is 'obvious' to one group of practitioners may be far from obvious to another. Research may be able to contribute to a resolution of such disagreements. This will not always be possible, though, because the necessary knowledge may not be available or easily accessible, even for researchers. Also, we must recognise that the resolution of such disagreements has to occur in a situation in which the various parties involved may have much to gain and lose depending on the outcome. This, combined with the inevitable residue of uncertainty surrounding scientific findings, often makes any consensual solution to the problem unlikely. This is true even outside the realm of social research. So, for example, when consumer groups, farmers and the Government turn to scientists to provide the necessary information to decide whether some food product should be withdrawn because of a health risk, there is only a small chance that scientists will be able to meet the situation in a way that will satisfy all sides; both because of the limitations of what they can offer and because of the political character of the situation. Where social research is involved, these problems are likely to be at least as serious and probably worse.

It should be clear from my account of the relationship between research and other forms of practice in Chapter 3, and from my comments here, that some clash of perspectives is to be expected between researchers and other practitioners. And, of course, this does occur. In my view, it is probably inevitable to some degree, because of the very different concerns of the two groups and the complex nature of both research and practice. However, the problem can be eased, I think, by recognising the differences between these two activities, and the limited but nevertheless valuable role that research can play in both the ways I have outlined. It is particularly important that research is not regarded as capable of replacing practical knowledge with prescriptions that simply have to be implemented for problems to be solved. In addition, though, I do believe that social research is currently neither sufficiently well funded *nor* sufficiently well organised to provide in full the sort of contribution to practice of which it is capable.[2]

ASSESSMENT OF RESEARCHERS

Sometimes assessment is concerned with the competence of the researchers. Here, some account must be taken of the circumstances in which the research was carried out: the limitations on resources, the contingencies of the research process, etc. It is often only too easy to identify the failings of particular ethnographic studies, and even to indicate strategies that could have been employed that might have improved the results. The reader is able to employ a hindsight that was not available to the researcher in the course of her or his research. This is especially important in the case of ethnographic research because it employs an exploratory and developmental approach in which the initial focus of the research may be transformed, and at the very least will be subject to clarification, over the course of the research. Furthermore, not only are there often severe resource constraints operating on researchers, but they also face trade-offs between different goals. For instance, one can usually only study a relatively small number of cases in depth, so that the detailed information about each case that this provides is usually bought at the expense of being less able to assess the generalisability of one's findings effectively. Similarly, if one makes heavy use of the accounts of informants one can cover more ground more rapidly than if one relies on participant observation; on the other hand, the use of informants adds new potential sources of error to the data. These are not either/or matters of course, many levels of trade-off are possible; but it is not always clear what the optimum level is, and our judgement about that may change over time as the research evolves.

What all this points to is that research is itself a form of practice, and what I said about the nature of practice in Chapter 5 applies just as much here as elsewhere. In particular, we must resist the temptation to see methodology as specifying a set of rules that can simply be applied to research practice. At best, it can only provide general guidance and there is much room for disagreement about what one can and cannot, should and should not, do on any particular occasion. Assessments of the research process where what is at issue is the competence of the researcher must take account of this. What I have focused on in this book is the judgement of ethnographic accounts against ideals. Important as that is, it cannot serve alone as a basis for fair assessments of researcher competence.

ASSESSING THE EFFECTIVENESS OF RESEARCH STRATEGIES

Another purpose that may motivate assessment is concern with the effectiveness of the research strategies employed in a study, with a view to judging the advantages and disadvantages of these strategies for future use. Whereas quantitative researchers have long been concerned with the development and assessment of particular research techniques – whether in the construction of attitude scales or modes of statistical analysis – ethnographers have shown less interest in this. In part this stems from the less structured character of ethnographic research, with its explicit concern to adapt to the circumstances being studied so as to minimise the researcher's effect and to modify the strategies employed in accordance with the developing research problem. From these points of view there is a sense in which all aspects of a piece of ethnographic research must be unique. However, this does not mean that we cannot identify common strategies employed by ethnographers, and make some assessment of them – as so long as we remember the practical character of ethnographic research and the resulting limitations of the contribution of methodology to it.

There is now a considerable prescriptive literature about ethnographic method, and this has come to be supplemented (as I have noted several times in this book) by research biographies.[3] Both types of literature involve informal assessments of particular research strategies drawing explicitly, and even more often implicitly, on the experience of the author and of other ethnographers. However, there has been rather little formal, collective assessment of strategies, building in a coordinated way on analysis of studies in which they have been used. An embryonic example of this sort of assessment can be found in Stephen Ball's biography of his research on Beachside Comprehensive school, where he examines the technique of respondent validation in the light of his own experience and the published account by Bloor of his use of it in studying ENT specialists (Ball, 1984; Bloor, 1978). However, such assessments rarely go very far or draw on the full range of literature available.

In making assessments of the effectiveness of particular strategies the likely validity of the research findings is an important consideration, but it is not the only one. A technique may be judged useful even though the findings of the studies in which it was used are not convincing, since that failure may arise from other factors. Conversely, even when the findings are convincing we may conclude that the research strategy is unlikely to be very effective in other circumstances.

ETHICS

An especially important dimension of the assessment of ethnographic research concerns ethics. We may often need to look at the techniques used in ethnographic research in terms of whether or not their use was legitimate. There have been many disputes about the ethics of particular ethnographic studies. (See the discussions in Becker, 1964; Filstead, 1970; Rynkiewich and Spradley, 1976; Reynolds, 1982, chapters 3 and 4 especially; Burgess, 1989.) These have tended to revolve around four issues: deception, privacy, consequences for others and for research.

1. Deception

This problem arises most strikingly in the case of covert research, where an ethnographer carries out research without most or all of the other participants being aware that research is taking place. Examples are Roy's research on workers in a machine shop and Homan's work on old time pentecostalists (Roy, 1952 and 1955; Homan, 1978).[4]

While the issue of deception is raised most sharply by covert research, it always arises to one degree or another. Ethnographers rarely tell the people they are studying *everything* about the research, partly because most of them are unlikely to want to know all the details, but also because of the danger that divulging information will affect their behaviour in ways that will invalidate the research. For instance, to tell teachers that one is interested in whether they normally talk as much to girls as to boys in the classroom may produce false results since they may make an effort to talk equally to both.[5] Roth has argued that all research falls on a continuum between the completely open and the completely covert (Roth, 1962); and it is worth emphasising that within the same piece of research the degree of openness may vary considerably among the various people in the field and over time.

2. Privacy

In everyday life we draw distinctions between public places (such as street corners) and private places (like the bedroom); as well as between information that is for public consumption and that which is secret or confidential. A frequent concern about ethnographic research is that it involves making public things said and done in private. Like deception, however, the concept of privacy is complex. What is public and what is private is rarely clear cut. Is the talk among people in a bar public or private? Does it make any difference if it is loud or *sotto voce?* We also seem to draw distinctions depending on who is involved. For instance, it is quite common for educational researchers to ask children about who their friends are, but it is very rare for them to investigate friendship patterns among teachers; and, in part, I think this stems from the assumption that children's private lives are open to scrutiny in a way that those of adults, especially professional, middle-class adults, are not. Also, privacy seems to be defined in terms of specific audiences that are and are not regarded as having legitimate access to information of particular kinds. (Not in front of the children; or not in front of the adults!) Sometimes, the invasion of privacy by researchers is justified on the grounds that since the account will be published for a specialised audience neither the people studied nor anyone else who knows them is likely to read it. But is this true? And, even if it is, does it excuse the invasion of privacy?

Social scientists have taken up contrasting positions about privacy and research. On the one hand, there are those who argue that the data which an ethnographer collects about a person, especially interview data, belong to that person, so that before they can be quoted in a research report permission for such quotation must be obtained.[6] At the other extreme there are those espousing what is sometimes called 'conflict methodology' who argue that researchers have a right, indeed an obligation, to investigate and to publish what they discover, especially when the subject of the research is people who are publicly accountable, or who ought to be (Rainwater and Pitman, 1967; Lehman and Young, 1974; Douglas, 1976; Lundman and McFarlane, 1976).

3. *Damaging consequences for others*

While ethnographic research rarely involves the sorts of damaging consequences that may be involved in, say, biological experiments on animals or the study of atomic reactions in physics, it can have important consequences both for the people studied and for others. For example, publication of an ethnographic account may harm the public reputation of individuals, groups or whole categories of people. A well-known example is the account of Springdale, a community in upper New York State, by Vidich and Bensman. Not only was this community recognised by some readers but a few of the individuals described were identifiable too (notably those playing leading roles in the community).[6] Another example that raises the same issue in a slightly different form is Ditton's study of 'fiddling and pilferage' among bread salesmen. He opens the preface to his book in the following way

I am lucky enough to have a number of friends and colleagues. Probably not as many of the former, and perhaps more of the latter now that this book has been published. I don't expect that many of the men at Wellbread's will look too kindly on the cut in real wages that this work may mean to them, and my bakery self would agree with them. (Ditton, 1977: vii)

4. *Consequences for future research*

Social researchers, and especially ethnographers, rely on being given access to settings by gatekeepers and others involved. Research that is found objectionable by the people studied and/or by gatekeepers may have the effect that these people refuse access to researchers in the future. If this were to happen on a large scale, research would become virtually impossible. This was one of the main arguments used by Fred Davis in his criticism of Lofland and Lejeune's covert study of a branch of Alcoholics Anonymous (Davis, 1961; Lofland and Lejeune, 1960; Lofland, 1961); and by Erickson against the covert study of an apocalyptic religious group in *When Prophecy Fails* (Festinger *et al.*, 1956; Erickson, 1967).

Summary

All of these are important considerations, though I am inclined to think that the third is the most important. However, as with all values the application of any one of them to a situation must be tempered by consideration of others, including the value of the research findings. Howard Becker claims that

(. . .) a good study of a community or organization must reflect the irreconcilable conflict between the interests of science and the interests of those studied, and thereby provoke a hostile reaction. (Becker, 1964: 276)

In my view this is an exaggeration, but it does point to the fallacy of any easy assumption that the researcher and the people studied will see the research in the same way. As in life generally, there may well be conflicting interpretations and conflicts of interest; and there are no simple general solutions to such conflicts. The ethical aspects of research, like others, must be viewed from a practical point of view. Take the value of honesty. It is certainly an important value, but that does not imply that we should always be absolutely honest. In everyday life, most of us do not tell the whole truth and nothing but the truth in all circumstances. We are circumspect about whom we tell what, and we may even lie on occasion: not only to protect our own interests but to protect those of others too, even those to whom we are lying. In my judgement we are right to apply this value selectively, and much the same applies in research. What is at issue is not 'to deceive or not to deceive' in abstract, but what and how much to tell whom on what occasion. And the same is true of the other three values. We must weigh the importance and contribution of the research against the chances and scale of any harm that is likely to be caused (to the people involved, to others, or to future access), against the value of honesty, and against any infringement of privacy involved. In the process, we shall find conflicting indications, difficult judgements and probably disagreements. Ethical issues are not matters on which simple and consensual decisions can always be made. Readers must try to make the most reasonable judgements they can, in the same way as must the researcher and the people studied; recognising that there can be legitimate differences of view. [8]

In order to illustrate the problems involved in making an assessment of the ethics of ethnographic studies, let me consider briefly the article of mine discussed in Chapter 6, this time looking at it from the point of view of ethics. This study undoubtedly involved deception of the teachers. While I had not specifically told them that I would only be researching classrooms, it seems likely that they would have concluded that this was the case. And I specifically did *not* tell them that I was collecting data in the staffroom because I feared that this would affect their behaviour, and might even lead them to refuse me continued access to the school. The question of privacy is also relevant since, by some definitions, what went on in the staffroom might be regarded as private. Certainly it was supposed to be private from the pupils: they were hardly ever allowed to come into that room. Parents and other people from outside the school were also not at liberty to enter the staffroom freely; and even the head seemed to feel himself something of an outsider in this setting. On the other hand, one might argue that the staffroom was a public setting for the teachers in relation to one another, certainly more so than their individual classrooms. And one might also claim that, as public servants, teachers should be open to such scrutiny.

The justification I used to myself at the time for engaging in deception and the invasion of privacy was that publication would not have damaging consequences for these teachers, and that the data collected there were important and could not have been obtained otherwise. I delayed publication to protect the teachers from identification. I have since been criticised for doing this on the grounds that I was, in effect, covering up racism. However, when I tried to publish my analysis of staffroom data in book form, one of the objections raised by the publisher's referees was that it represented a scurrilous attack on the teaching profession. [9]

My current view of the ethics of this study is that my judgement at the time was basically sound, but that the material should have been published earlier. It was very unlikely that the school and teachers would have been identified, and so there was little danger of damage being done to their reputations or careers. The publication of the account might possibly have damaged the standing of teachers in general, but this seems very unlikely given that it was presented as a study of a small number of teachers in one school; though the atypicality of that school was only emphasised in the thesis, not in the article. In my view, the deception and invasion of privacy were minimal and justified, despite the fact that my assessment of the value of the study is now a good deal lower than it was at the time I completed it.

You may or may not agree with my conclusions about the ethics of this piece of ethnography, and by no means all ethnographers would.

But the discussion does illustrate something of the way in which factual and value judgements have to be combined and weighed against one another when making an ethical assessment of ethnographic studies.

CONCLUSION

This book has been primarily concerned with the task of assessing the value of particular ethnographic accounts from the point of view of their contribution to the research literature. I have outlined an approach to this task in some detail and illustrated its application. In this final chapter I have discussed some other aspects of the process of reading and assessing ethnographic research. I have looked briefly at assessments by practitioners, judgements of the competence of researchers, and discussions of the effectiveness and ethics of particular research techniques. In closing this book I want to reiterate what I said in the Preface about the importance of the reading and assessment of research in the social science community. There is a tendency in ethnographic methodology to emphasise the doing of research, either in naive realist terms of discovering reality or in anti-realist terms of the artistry of the ethnographer. In this book I have sought to redress the balance somewhat by emphasising the important role that the reading and assessment of ethnographic research should play. In Chapter 5 I noted that ethnographic studies are not well coordinated with one another (or with other sorts of research). While reference is made to other research to justify the focus and to support or elaborate the analysis and the conclusions drawn, each study tends to be viewed as a piece of solo virtuosity that must stand on its own. And the preponderant justification given for studies is that they open up new areas of investigation. Much less effort has been put into the checking and extension of previous accounts and the development and testing of existing theoretical ideas. Perhaps if more attention were given to the assessment of studies this would lead to more concerted efforts on the part of ethnographers in these respects, and thereby to more rapid progress in the production of valid and relevant sociological knowledge. That, at least, is the hope on which this book is founded.

NOTES

1. By the term 'practitioner' I mean a person engaged in any activity, any practice, other than research.
2. My view is rather different to that promoted by those favouring practitioner research. I am not denying that research of some kinds may usefully be carried out by practitioners, nor that this may

sometimes produce more valuable results than those generated by specialist research. However, it is no panacea. See Hammersley and Scarth (1990).

3. For a guide to this literature, see the annotated bibliography in Hammersley and Atkinson (1983).

4. See Bulmer (1982b) for a collection of articles discussing the ethics of covert research.

5. Of course, in action research this may not matter. Indeed, the aim may be to see how far behaviour can be changed. See Alison Kelly's discussion of this aspect of the Girls into Science and Technology project (Kelly, 1985).

6. MacDonald (1974) and Walker (1974). See also Jenkins (n.d.).

7. Vidich and Bensman (1958). For discussion of the ethical issues, see Vidich and Bensman (1964) and Becker (1964).

8. The idea that there may be irreconcilable conflict between values receives its classic treatment in some of the writings of Max Weber, notably Weber (1958). For a more recent and detailed discussion, see Larmore (1987).

9. Parts have been published in article form. Besides that included in Appendix 1, see Hammersley (1981).

Staffroom news

In the past twenty years a considerable body of ethnographic research has been carried out in schools. The bulk of this has focused on classrooms. Such a focus is not unreasonable, of course, since the classroom is the place where one might expect the most important work of the school to take place. But there is much to be learned from looking at other parts of schools, and indeed at other aspects of schooling, than teacher–pupil interaction.

One important but neglected area is the structure of social relationships to be found among teachers.[1] This is a key issue in itself from the point of view of the sociology of occupations, but, of course, staff relations are also likely to be a significant factor shaping what occurs in the classroom. This article looks at one aspect of relations among the teaching staff of a small, inner-city, boys' secondary modern school (to which I have given the pseudonym 'Downtown'). It focuses on the exchange of 'news' about pupils in the staffroom and seeks to identify its functions.[2]

In the morning, before school starts, the teachers at Downtown sit or stand around in the staffroom reading papers, chatting and smoking. At dinnertime they eat in the hall with the pupils and then come to the staffroom; or eat sandwiches in the staffroom and stay there until afternoon lessons begin, talking, playing cards, etc. During free periods they read newspapers, chat with whoever happens to be there, or mark books.

While there was some variation in who sat where, there were informal groups centred on each of the three coffee tables in the staffroom. For much of the time the three tables formed self-contained interaction groups, although the staffroom as a whole was occasionally the audience. At other times, smaller standing or sitting groups straddling the usual groups were formed.

The typical distribution of the teachers across the three tables partly reflected friendship networks, but the tables were also sites for different activities. Table 1 was invariably occupied with bridge at lunchtime and sometimes at break. Table 2 was often a solo whist game at lunchtime. A regular member of Table 3 mentioned that at one time they had done crosswords though during the period of fieldwork they merely talked, ate sandwiches and read newspapers.

Talk was undoubtedly the major staffroom activity, ranging in focus from football to classical music. However, most staffroom conversation was shop talk, and usually about Downtown and its pupils.

TYPES OF STAFFROOM NEWS

A consequence of the structure of the teachers' work situation at Downtown is that while the information acquired by one in the course of his work is likely to be different from that acquired by others, it is nevertheless of potential relevance to the whole staff. This arises in particular from the fact that, because classes move around between them, the teachers all face the same pupils at one time or another. A premium is thereby placed on the gathering and trading of 'news' about pupils.

Some of this 'news' is about specific events:

1 (Greaves enters the staffroom and speaks to the whole room)
  Greaves: Don't anybody hit Storey for a bit, lay off Storey for a week or so everyone.
  T: Why?
  Greaves: His mother's just been in.
  T: What happened?
  Greaves: She came up to me an' said 'I'll push yer glasses through yer face'.
  T: What did you say?
  Greaves: I raised myself up to my full height and said: 'Madam, if you have a complaint you must see the headmaster' and I walked down to the office with her muttering behind me. Anyway, the head saw her off. He told me to hit him on the shoulder in the future, where it doesn't mark. I haven't heard of that before.
  Webster: That's what Freddy Carpenter used to do, lay about the shoulder (*laughter*).
  T: Aye, after he'd kicked them in the crutch.
  (Greaves mentioned that the mother had said that someone else had hit him on Monday)
  Baldwin: I think I hit him yesterday.
  Denison: I kicked him out.
  T: I don't think he went up to games.
  Baldwin: Oh well I can't have hit him then, my conscience is clear.
  Denison: Well, I kicked him out (*laughter*). Oh no, not literally, I think he did go up to games.
  Baldwin: Oh don't say that.
  (At lunchtime Greaves tells the story again, this time

mentioning that Storey's mother was accompanied by another woman)

T: For support I suppose.

T: What did you do to him?

Greaves: Oh I hit him across the face three times – he reckons he counted five as his head hit the desk.

T: What had he done?

Greaves: Oh you know what Storey's like, he's one of those lads who acts just at the wrong moment, he goes just too far, just tips the balance.

On other occasions there is a pooling of news about the same event from multiple sources, including information gleaned from the pupils themselves:

2   (Staffroom) There is talk about a fight that had taken place in the hall, a prefect had hit three fourth year pupils and one of the latter had tried to hit the prefect in the face with a piece of slate (there are builders in the school). The prefect put his hand up to prevent this and his hand was cut. There was much talk about why the prefect had hit the pupils. I think the teachers were in a quandary. On the one hand, he was apparently provoked, on the other prefects are not supposed to inflict physical punishment. One teacher says 'The head is very concerned and came into the classroom and gave the 5th form a rollicking without mentioning the prefect by name'. Another points out that they had had trouble with that form (the fifth form) when it had been a third form. Holton asks: 'Who got the best of it?' There's a discussion between Webster and Denison (the latter very concerned about likely repercussions on the prefect). Webster reports that 'There's a rumour among the boys that a fourth year gang are going to get the prefect, forty of them, it's no joke, they could disable a teacher'. Some comments were also made to the effect that the prefects represented the teachers.

Staffroom news is selected and presented in terms of its relevance to common problems and issues. The two extracts just quoted are clear examples of this. Thus in Extract 1 the account of the irate mother is prefaced by a summary of its implications for colleagues: 'Lay off Storey for a while.' Furthermore, this account relates to some major teacher worries: possible interference by parents, and being prosecuted for hitting pupils. The former concern has been well-documented elsewhere (Becker, 1951; Sharp and Green, 1975; Lortie, 1975) and emerges clearly in this example; the latter came out quite explicitly at other times in the staffroom:

3   (Staffroom: Larson to Walker in MH's presence)
Larson: You ought to be official NUT Convenor.
Walker: I'm only in the NUT for one reason.
(Larson looks significantly towards MH)
Larson: In case you get prosecuted for hitting someone.
Walker: That's right.

While the news about the fight in Extract 2 does not include any specific guidance for future action, it too is relevant to a prevailing staff concern: the danger of pupil violence towards teachers. If the pupils can hit a prefect, a representative of the teachers, might they not start attacking the teachers themselves? While as far as I could tell this had never happened, the possibility was mentioned several times in the staffroom and seemed to underly much talk about the pupils:

4   Webster: I don't know what'll happen this term, it'll be a matter of containment, it's the last two days I'm worried about.
Dixon: We'll be issued with guns for the last two days, Thompson submachine guns mounted on our desks.

5   (Talk about Wilson (a pupil) between Baldwin and MH after a lesson)
Baldwin: When you face him his chin's up here (about nose level) and I'm fairly tall, it's quite alarming in a physical sense. I wouldn't like to control him for another two years.

This concern about the danger of pupil violence perhaps explains the staff's somewhat ambivalent attitude towards the prefect and his actions in Extract 2. On the one hand, as their representative, he should be respected by the pupils, and to ensure this he must be supported in his dealings with them; just as a teacher must be supported by his colleagues, and in particular by the head (Becker, 1951). On the other hand, the teachers were clearly concerned that this prefect's possibly illegitimate action might itself actually spark off physical attacks on teachers.

Much staffroom news though is not about specific events at all. Some, for example, concerns pupil moods:

6   (Staffroom)
Webster: 4T are playing up today.

7   (Staffroom)
Greaves: I don't know what's happened but 3T are working this morning.

8   (Staffroom:Webster to Marsden)
Webster: What mood's (name) in today?

Who's here and who's absent are also reported; though it is only the presence and absence of 'problem' pupils which seems to be newsworthy:

9 T: All the clowns in that form are away at the moment, (name) was being very stupid.

10 T: Donald Channing has been put into detention centre.
    Greaves: Good. Has Hughes been excluded because of window breaking?
    T: No, because of the nurse.
    Greaves: Oh pity, that means he'll come back. Still I suppose we should be thankful for small mercies.

11 (Denison and Webster) Denison recounts who in a particular class is away to indicate that it won't be too bad taking 3T. Webster tells how he tried to persuade a pupil to bunk off (i.e. to truant).

12 Greaves: O'Brien's been suspended.
    T: Where from?
    T: By the neck I hope.

13 Webster: (Aldwych) is back, horrible child.

Once again this news is closely tied to classroom concerns and is made relevant by the fact that the pupils pass round from one teacher to another for different lessons. Given the assumption that there are certain 'prime-movers', getting such information may enable a teacher to anticipate how a lesson will go and what problems are likely to arise.

The primary concern underlying all this news is with sources of trouble and the most common kind of staffroom news retains this interest while being even further removed from specific events. Here teachers' current characterizations of problem pupils are exchanged:

14 (Philipson and Baldwin talking about 2T)
    Baldwin: There's seven good lads but there's some little buggers: Short, Cook, Mills, Dunn's top of the list. Arnold's vicious, aggressive, resentful. . .
    Philipson: (*laughing*) Is that all?
    Baldwin: Richardson, I can get along with him, he's just a bit loud that's all.
    Philipson: Gary's not so bad.
    Baldwin: He's easily led that's his trouble, get no pleasure out of taking 2T, no pleasure at all, I get more pleasure out of teaching third year classes.

15 (Staffroom):
    Webster: (Name), he's an oaf.
    Walker: Well y'know why, he's stupid, can't even read or write.
    Webster: O'Brien's going off his head.
    MH: (*Laughs*)
    Webster: It's not just an expression, I mean it, he's going off his head, but nobody does anything about it of course.

What we have here is the trading of summary typifications of pupils.[3] Teachers employ typifications of pupils to guide their actions (Rist, 1973; Hargreaves, Hester and Mellor, 1975). 'Knowing what to expect' from different quarters minimises the cues required to come to some conclusion about what is going on, what is about to happen, who is involved, in what role, and what can be done about it. Knowing what 'type' a pupil is is important, otherwise one might be caught unawares. Teachers' reliance on typifications is heightened by the immediacy of the classroom (Jackson, 1968; Doyle, 1977) and their responsibility for what goes on there. Yet, at the same time, these features of classroom interaction also minimise the evidence available for the construction of typifications. Given this, it is perhaps not surprising that the teachers at Downtown seem to supplement their own observations with information from colleagues.

TEACHERS' TYPIFICATIONS OF PUPILS

There is now a considerable literature on teacher typifications (Hargreaves, 1977). The impetus for this derived initially from the concept of the self-fulfilling prophecy (Merton, 1957), dramatically and controversially demonstrated in the classroom by Rosenthal and Jacobson (1968).[4] Their experimental approach has been followed up by more ethnographic work, notably that of Rist (1970, 1973), Nash (1973) and Sharp and Green (1975). More recently, however, attention has shifted somewhat, away from the consequentiality of teacher typifications for pupil careers, and towards an examination of their structure and process. Thus, for example, Leiter (1974) investigated the processes by which kindergarten children are assigned to different ability groups within the class and to different classes in the first grade. In doing this he focuses on the structure of social interaction in assessment interviews and assignment meetings, and the typifications and criteria involved in the decisions. Similarly, but this time in the field of secondary education, Hargreaves *et al.* (1975) have developed a complex model of the process by which pupils are typed as deviant and how these types underpin teachers' responses to classroom events.

Most research in this area to date has sought to identify the typifications used by teachers in the classroom or other assessment settings. While the importance of the staffroom as a place where teachers 'compare notes' about pupils has been recognised (Hargreaves, 1972, chapter 12; Hargreaves *et al.*, 1975, pp. 62–5), the nature of such discussions has not been investigated. But the analysis of staffroom typifications has methodological as well as substantive significance. Existing research on typifications has relied almost entirely on interview data, and questions inevitably arise about the relationship between the typifications elicited in that context and those which are actually operative in the classroom. After all if, as is generally accepted, action is always tailored to the situation in which it occurs, this is no less true of interview talk than of action in any other setting. How much, then, do the typifications elicited owe to the interview context itself? There is no basis for claiming that staffroom talk about pupils is any closer to classroom operative typifications than that elicited in interviews; but it does provide us with another source of evidence.

Crucial to the nature of both staffroom typifications and those elicited in interviews is that they are two-stage productions. In the classroom the teachers are constantly monitoring and making sense of pupil behaviour, and the products of this process are sedimented as typificatory knowledge. We can expect that this material is then reworked to one degree or another to produce staffroom typifications. Unfortunately, there is no direct way of identifying the nature of this production process and how it differs from that involved in interviews. One indirect line of attack, however, is to compare the typifications produced in the two types of context. Thus, for example, one can compare the staffroom typifications reported here with those elicited in interviews by Hargreaves *et al.* (1975).

At a superficial level, at least, the *content* of the typifications produced in the two contexts does not seem all that different. They are both structured around what are generally regarded as the two basic classroom concerns of teachers: order and learning (Stebbins, 1975, p. 45). Even though in both sets of data general descriptors are used much of the time (e.g. in Example 14 'good', 'little buggers', 'vicious', 'aggressive', etc.) it is quite clear that the typifications are formulated in terms of how much trouble the pupil is for the teachers: 'I can get along with him', 'I get no pleasure out of taking 2T . . . '. There may, of course, be more subtle differences in the way in which these themes are handled in the two kinds of data; and indeed my subsequent analysis of staffroom talk will suggest that this is likely to be the case.

In one respect typifications in the two contexts are strikingly different. Those reported by Hargreaves *et al.* (1975) are extensive and elaborated, those exchanged in the Downtown staffroom highly abbreviated. An explanation for this immediately suggests itself on the basis of the nature of the two contexts. Where interaction between the same participants is recurrent, processes of routinisation and institutionalisation occur and interaction becomes more economic; much is taken for granted as no longer needing to be spelt out (Berger and Luckmann, 1967). On the other hand, in interactions with relative strangers, and especially strangers who occupy a strange and ill-defined role such as that of researcher, much will be spelt out at length, especially when the researcher encourages long, open-ended responses.[5]

Underlying some staffroom news is a standard set of pupil types. Sometimes the pupils are described as unpredictable and dangerous:

16 Webster: Wilson, he's going to kill someone one day, he's got the killer instinct. How he's changed, you can see the mentality breaking up, he's unstable.

   Denison: You should have seen him loping across the road at four o'clock yesterday, like a prehistoric animal.

On other occasions they are simply 'buggers', 'bastards', 'yobos' or 'louts', showing little respect for authority and often setting out to cause trouble:

17 (Staffroom)
   Greaves: His balls haven't dropped yet and he's the worst bastard I've had to deal with in eighteen years teaching.

Perhaps the key feature of the 'unstable' and the 'lout'[6] is that there is little a teacher can do to change them; he must simply recognise how they are and deal with them accordingly, for example by avoiding confrontations:

18 (Staffroom)
   Denison: You've got to try and avoid confrontations, although they sometimes force confrontations on you. (He later explained how he had spent twenty minutes telling a class off today.) You could spend all your time trying to persuade or force the reluctant to work, if there are some who are willing to work it's better to concentrate on them.

However, there are some pupils who appear to be louts but are actually more manageable: they are simply 'easily led':

19 (Staffroom)
   Philipson: Gary's not so bad.
   Baldwin: He's easily led that's his trouble.

These three types of pupil relate primarily to the concern with classroom order and possible pupil violence towards teachers. They each pose a threat, though the third is the weak link, the one where pressure may work. Other problem pupils pose more of a nuisance than a threat, they are 'immature':

20 (Classroom talk between Denison and MH after a lesson)
    Denison: (Name's) an immature lad, cards stuffed in his pockets.

The 'immature' do not challenge teacher authority in any serious or effective way, nor are they physically dangerous. Their deviance is simply an irritation, and results primarily from intrinsic interest in 'childish' activities that are proscribed by school rules.

However, despite these standard types, the nature of the pupils is not treated as static, and much news concerns changes in the pupils, almost always for the worse:

21 Holton: Has Mills been suspended then?
    Roach: Well he's here this morning.
    Holton: Oh so he's not been suspended, after all the head's great threats. It's funny that lad should have gone that way in the last few months. Nobody had ever heard of him before, I mean he's been here four years, someone must have heard of him, y'know as an odd fellow, but not for creating violence.

22 (Marsden about a pupil to other teachers in the staffroom)
    Marsden: He's getting worse, he needs taking to the head, that'd do him good.

23 (Staffroom discussion)
    Holton: I'll tell you who's becoming a very silly lad: X (pupil's name).
    Scott: I pointed that out a few weeks ago, he should be put in front of the head, it's a phase.
    Holton: Everything Jerry Roach (student teacher) told him to do he did in the most silly, stupid way.
    Scott: (And yet) he's potentially one of the best lads, potentially way beyond the rest.
    Holton: The intelligence is there but he will constantly do the wrong thing.

24 (Staffroom discussion)
    Webster: I'll tell you who's turning nasty: Gary.
    Walker: Johns you mean, well that's because he's stupid, he can't read or write. He reminds me of something in an African jungle.

There is considerable agreement on a list of the infamous, but the list changes over time, stars rise and fall.[7]

An important feature of staffroom news at Downtown is the predominant concern with the 'behaviour' of pupils; in other words with those features of them relevant to the problem of maintaining 'order' in the classroom. Only a few staffroom comments included in the data relate to the 'ability' of pupils and their response' to teaching:

25 Philipson: O'Brien is in the top set in Maths.
Baldwin: (to Philipson) Has O'Brien got anything upstairs?
Philipson: No, neither has (name), he got an E in the test, oh n'then a B I think.
T: He doesn't even know his three times table.
T: Most of them don't.
Denison: Some of them don't even know how many inches in a foot.

26 Webster: (Name), he's so lazy it takes him twenty minutes to pick up the pencil and twenty minutes to put it down. (Name) looks prehistoric, I wonder if he's on drugs.

27 Webster: Gibbs is dead to the world.

In summary, then, while some staffroom news is concerned with specific events or the moods, presences and absences of particular pupils, most of it reports how the teachers are finding particular pupils troublesome in the classroom and what conclusions they have come to about what can be expected from them. What is involved here is a process of collective sense-making and stock-taking.

THE RHETORICAL FUNCTIONS OF STAFFROOM NEWS

It must not be assumed, however, that typifications necessarily have a purely referential function. In the Downtown staffroom, typifications of pupils are frequently used in a more rhetorical fashion than the idea of 'comparing notes' or 'stock-taking' suggests, being dismissive as much as descriptive:

28 Webster: They're all louts.

29 (Staffroom)
Baldwin: X (pupil's name) is bright.
Denison: Potentially, but he's got a quirk.
Baldwin: They've all got their quirks I suppose.
Denison: But his quirks are between wider extremes, he's got a nice side and a nasty side. Most of them have just got quirks within the nasty.
Marsden: The rest of them come to school to be nasty.
Baldwin: They are nasty.
(Also, see Examples 14, 15, 16, 17, 20, 25, 26, and 27)

Both the form and the content of the accounts given in the staffroom seem to be shaped to this rhetorical function. For example, a striking feature of staffroom news about pupils is that it generally concentrates on the nature of particular pupils rather than describing their actions in detail; and even where their actions are reported these are described without reference to the features of the particular interactional context in which they occurred.

30   Vaughan: Mills went berserk this morning, he's a bit unstable that lad.

31   Vaughan: Mills really blew his top today. He'll be inside soon I know it, he's going that way.

32   Vaughan: Mills is going to end up on a manslaughter charge.

33   Vaughan: The slightest thing can set him (Mills) off, someone's only got to stand on his toe and he's off.

34   (Vaughan talks about Mills now and last year)
       Vaughan: If he can't conform reasonably to society then society'll have to kick him out and treat him as an exceptional case.
       Philipson: He's got a tremendous persecution complex.

According to all these descriptions, this pupil is liable to explode at any time for no reason at all, 'the slightest thing can set him off'! This is reminiscent of some of Dorothy Smith's (1978) data, and her analysis of the selective contextualisation involved in the story 'K is mentally ill' told by Angela, 'one of the girls':

'Nearly every morning K would cry in the car, being upset about little things, and the girls would comfort her.'
   In this instance, the reasons for K's crying are taken to be those immediate occasions which were directly observable to 'the girls' and which were 'little things', not sufficient to warrant her weeping. Angela does not raise the possibility that there might have been features of K's biography unknown to her and the others which would provide adequate reasons for K's disposition to cry so readily.
   Accordingly, also it is not a problem or ought not to be a problem for the reader/hearer who properly follows the instructions for how the account is to be read, that no explanation, information, etc., from K is introduced at any point in the account. And it is not or ought not to be strange that at no point is there any mention of K being asked to explain, inform, etc.
   In sum, then, the rules, norms, information, observations, etc., presented by the teller of the tale are to be treated by the reader/hearer as the only warranted set. (Smith, 1978, p. 35)

This 'cutting out' of context occurs in staffroom talk at Downtown even where the events concerned have had important consequences and where a teacher is specifically asked 'what happened' by a colleague (see Example 1 above). In all the examples of staffroom talk I collected,[8] the setting, including the actions of the teacher, is taken for granted as natural and normal and as warranting certain behaviour. For the teachers the occurrence of that behaviour does not require explanation, and indeed it does not normally constitute staffroom news. What is a recurrent topic for comment and discussion in the staffroom is the 'failure' of pupils to conform to those expectations.

The rhetorical function of staffroom news can also be detected in the kinds of explanation implied in the typifications. For the most part these appeal to psychological characteristics of pupils: moods, characters and mental disorder. Thus, in the case of Mills quoted above (in Examples 30–4), there is apparently something about him, or in him, which makes him 'unstable' and results in him beng unable to 'conform reasonably'. Moreover, it seems (see Example 21 above) that this aspect of his nature has 'emerged' relatively recently and if it continues he will 'end up on a manslaughter charge' and go 'inside'. In the teacher's account Mills' 'condition' has its own dynamic. All of the psychological characteristics attributed to pupils in these teacher typifications, then, are presented as underlying generative features which produce typical behaviour in diverse contexts; indeed irrespective of the context. Nor is there any attempt to trace the causation of these features, to ask why the pupils have these moods, for example, or why Mills might have a persecution complex. Even the notion of behavioural contagion, a more sociological theory (Sutherland, 1956), is psychologised: some pupils are simply 'easily led'.

There has been some discussion in the literature of the 'ideological' role of psychological explanations, notably in individualising failure, explaining it in terms of the characteristics of the individual rather than in terms of the structure of society (Ingleby, 1976; Bowles and Gintis, 1976).[9] But, even if the form of explanation employed by the teachers at Downtown does indeed fulfil some larger social function, we must still ask why they adopt it. We cannot assume it is simply because they have the interests of the system at heart. While remote causes may well be involved, these would operate through more proximal phenomena and it is these which are my concern here.

In discussing teachers' reactions to badly behaved and below average pupils, Stebbins (1975, p. 64) suggests the following explanation for the common tendency to blame the pupil:

There is something disquieting about these students to their teachers; despite their often exceptional efforts to instill respect for classroom rules and raise levels of achievement, the latter still fail. Teachers can blame only two sources for their lack of success: themselves or others. As in other conventional occupations, they choose the latter alternative and thus contend that there is an important aspect of the students' lives or personalities affecting their behavior at school which is beyond their (the teachers') ability to manipulate.

This seems a plausible explanation for the nature of the typifications of pupils that Downtown teachers exchange in the staffroom. But we must ask why it is that these teachers are faced with the choice of blaming either themselves or their pupils. After all, they might equally appeal to the conditions in which they are forced to work or to the nature of the society in which they live as the source of their, and their pupils', problems. To understand why they do not do this I think we have to look at the conception of teaching to which Downtown teachers are committed. Theirs is a very traditional approach to pedagogy, according to which teaching is a skill which one either has or does not have:

> 35   (Staffroom: Walker and Baldwin talking about resources)
>   Baldwin: Sarge and I calculated we needed £700.
>   Walker: I couldn't spend £200. Whatever the school it's the teacher that's important, it doesn't matter what books and equipment there are if the teacher's no good.
>   Webster: A good teacher can teach in a henhouse.
>   Walker: Whatever the school you must teach basically the same material: the basic skills.

In these terms any failure on the part of pupils to 'behave' and 'learn' is the product either of teacher incompetence or of the ignorance, stupidity and/or loutishness of pupils. From this point of view, the characteristics of the pupils referred to in staffroom news represent obstacles to be recognised, not problems that can be solved by the adoption of appropriate methods. In fact, the explanations for pupil behaviour implied in Downtown teachers' typifications of their pupils are not strictly speaking explanations at all, they have the form of predictions and function as excuses (Lyman and Scott, 1970). They specify dangers and limits involved in teaching Downtown pupils, rather than being concerned with identifying problems and finding strategies for solving them.

The construction of descriptions of pupils which cut out the context of their behaviour, and the kinds of explanation for pupils' behaviour employed, both operate to explain away poor pupil performances as the product of ineducability. Through trading news in the staffroom about their pupils Downtown teachers defend their collective sense of competence in the face of potentially discrediting evidence.

CONCLUSION

I have argued that one important function of staffroom news at Downtown is a kind of collective stocktaking in which teachers compare notes and bring themselves up to date about the pupils whom they all face in the classroom. However, this does not provide an entirely satisfactory explanation for the nature of this staffroom news. The form and content of the accounts of pupils which the teachers exchange suggests that they also serve a rhetorical function. They seem to be designed to protect the teachers' professional identities in the face of the threat to their sense of their own competence posed by the behaviour of the pupils. However, it is important to remember that this threat derives in part from the teachers' commitment to 'traditional' teaching. Moreover, the process of collective self-protection which underpins the exchange of staffroom news at Downtown serves at the same time to preserve this commitment from pressure for change.

NOTES

1. There has been some empirical research in this area. See Lortie (1975), Woods (1979a) and Hitchcock (1983). For valuable, though speculative, discussions see Waller (1967) and Hargreaves (1972) and (1980).
2. Other aspects of staff relations at Downtown are discussed in Hammersley (1980).
3. For the most part these fall into Becker's (1952) categories of relevance to 'teaching' and 'discipline'. Only one example seems to relate simply to what Becker calls 'moral acceptability':

   Webster: You can smell him two classrooms off.

4. Rosenthal and Jacobson's results have been challenged. See Good and Brophy (1978) for a useful discussion.
5. On this interpretation my evidence is compatible with that of Hargreaves *et al.* (1975). However, this does not necessarily suggest that their findings actually reflect teachers' classroom typifications. It may reflect instead some correspondence at another level between staffroom and interview talk. In fact, elsewhere Hargreaves (1977) actually suggests such a correspondence, dubbing it 'third party talk'. Woods (1979a) also questions the relationship between the kinds of typifications documented by Hargreaves *et al.* (1975) and teachers' classroom practices. In addition, he provides some data which do not fit the superficial contrast I have drawn between staffroom and interview data. He presents an interview transcript in which the typifications are highly abbreviated. However, there is a possible, and plausible, explanation for this which leaves my argument substantially intact. This is that the distinction between staffroom and interview contexts is analytically unsatisfactory. What is crucial is not the way settings are conventionally defined but how actors actually define them. I suggest that perhaps in Woods' interview the informant treated him as a colleague as much as a researcher, and that this shaped the nature of his response. This fits Woods' account of his research strategy, in Woods (1977) and

(1979a). Regarding the more fundamental issue of the relationship between any of these data and the typifications used by teachers in the classroom, at the moment we are simply in the dark.

6. It is of some interest that these two categories of pupil closely parallel some accounts of pupil and youth typifications. Thus 'the mentally unstable' seems to match the 'nutter' among football fans (Marsh, Rosser and Harre, 1978), the 'louts' are perhaps similar to Willis's 'lads' (Willis, 1977).

7. See Hargreaves' (1967) account of the rise and fall of reputations among pupils. I am not suggesting that teachers' perceptions of the rise and fall of pupils as 'louts' will be an accurate representation of reputations among the pupils, though there may be some relation. Note, however, that the two reputations interact (there may of course be more than two). While a pupil's reputation among teachers will be related to his actions, teachers' actions affect pupil reputations and pupil choices of courses of action. While Hargreaves does not mention this, and it goes against his argument in that he seems to see the pupil subculture as autonomous, once established, evidence for this interaction can be found in his account of the beginning of Clint's rise to become 'Cock of the School'.

8. For a discussion of the problems involved in assessing the representativeness of these data, see Hammersley (1984).

9. However, frequently the falsity of psychological explanations is taken for granted. While I think it can be quite satisfactorily demonstrated that there are social structural conditions for 'success', psychological attributes no doubt also play a role in determining who 'succeeds' and who 'fails'. One should not simply reject a form of explanation on the grounds of unpalatable political implications.

REFERENCES

Abraham, J. (1989) 'Testing Hargreaves' and Lacey's differentiation–polarisation theory in a setted comprehensive', *British Journal of Sociology*, **40**, 1, pp. 46–81.

Anderson, R., Hughes, J. and Sharrock, W. (1986) *Philosophy and the Human Sciences,* London, Croom Helm.

Anyon, J. (1981) 'Social class and school knowledge', *Curriculum Inquiry*, **11**, 1, pp. 3–42.

Aristotle (1976) *Ethics*, Harmondsworth, Penguin.

Arnold, D. (1970) (ed.) *Subcultures*, Berkeley, Glendessary Press.

Athens, L. (1984) 'Scientific criteria for evaluating qualitative studies', in N. K. Denzin (ed.) *Studies in Symbolic Interaction*, vol. 5, Greenwich, JAI Press.

Atkinson, M. (1984) *Our Masters' Voices*, London, Methuen.

Atkinson, P. (1975) 'In cold blood: bedside teaching in a medical school', in G. Chanan and S. Delamont (eds) *Frontiers of Classroom Research*, Windsor, National Foundation for Educational Research.

Atkinson, P. (1981a) *The Clinical Experience: the construction and reconstruction of medical reality*, Farnborough, Gower.

Atkinson, P. (1981b) personal communication.

Atkinson, P. (1982) 'Writing ethnography', in H. J. Helle (ed.) *Kultur und Institution*, Berlin, Dunker und Humblot, pp. 77–105.

Atkinson, P. (1990) *The Ethnographic Imagination*, London, Routledge.

Atkinson, P., Delamont, S. and Hammersley, M. (1988) 'Qualitative research traditions: a British response', *Review of Educational Research*, **58**, 2, pp. 231–50

Atkinson, P., Shone, D. and Rees, T. (1981) 'Labouring to learn? Industrial training for slow learners', in L. Barton and S. Tomlinson (eds) *Special Education: policy, practices and social issues*, London, Harper and Row.

Ball, S. J. (1981) *Beachside Comprehensive: a case study of schooling*, Cambridge, Cambridge University Press.

Ball, S. J. (1984) 'Beachside reconsidered: reflections on a methodological apprenticeship', in R. G. Burgess (ed.)

Bateson, G. (1958) (2nd edition) *Naven: the culture of the Iatmul people of New Guinea as revealed through a study of the 'naven' ceremonial*, Stanford, Stanford University Press.

Beattie, G. (1984) *Talk: an analysis of speech and non-verbal behaviour in conversation*, Milton Keynes, Open University Press.

Becker, H. S. (1951) *Role and Career Problems of the Chicago Public School Teacher*, PhD dissertation, University of Chicago.

Becker, H. S. (1952) 'Social class variations in the teacher–pupil relationship', *Journal of Educational Sociology*, **25**, No. 4.

Becker, H. S. (1964) 'Problems in the publication of field studies', in Vidich, Bensman and Stein (eds).

Becker, H. S. (1966) 'Introduction' to the reprint of C. Shaw (1930).

Becker, H. S. (1970) *Sociological Work*, Chicago, Aldine.

Becker, H. S., Geer, B., Hughes, E. C. and Strauss, A. (1961) *Boys in White*, Chicago, University of Chicago Press.

Becker, H. S., Geer, B., Hughes, E. C. and Strauss, A. (1969) *Making the Grade*, New York, Wiley.

Bell, C. and Newby, H. (1971) *Community Studies*, London, Allen and Unwin.

Berger, P. and Luckmann, T. (1967) *The Social Construction of Reality*, London, Allen Lane.

Black, M. (1967) 'Induction', in P. Edwards (ed.) *The Encyclopedia of Philosophy*, vol. 4, New York, Macmillan.

Bloor, M. (1978) 'On the analysis of observational data: a discussion of the worth and uses of inductive techniques and respondent validation', *Sociology*, **12**, 3, pp. 545–7.

Blumer, H. (1939) *Critiques of Research in the Social Sciences: I An Appraisal of Thomas and Znaniecki's 'The Polish Peasant in Europe and America'*, New York, Social Science Research Council.

Blumer, H. (1969) *Symbolic Interactionism*, Englewood Cliffs, Prentice Hall.

Bowles, S. and Gintis, H. (1976) *Schooling in Capitalist America,* London, Routledge and Kegan Paul,

Brophy, J. and Good, T. (1970) 'Teachers' communications of differential expectations for children's classroom performance: some behavioral data', *Journal of Educational Psychology*, **61**, 5, pp. 365–74.

Brown, R. (1977) *A Poetic for Sociology*, Cambridge, Cambridge University Press.

Bruyn, S. (1966) *The Human Perspective in Sociology: the methodology of participant observation*, Englewood Cliffs, Prentice Hall.

Bulmer, M. (1982a) *The Uses of Social Research: social investigation in public policy-making*, London, Allen and Unwin.

Bulmer, M. (1982b) *Social Research Ethics*, London, Macmillan.

Bulmer, M. (1984) *The Chicago School of Sociology*, Chicago, University of Chicago Press.

Burawoy, M. (1985) *The Politics of Production: factory regimes under capitalism and socialism*, London, Verso.

Burgess, R. G. (1982) *Field Research: a sourcebook and field manual*, London, Allen and Unwin.

Burgess, R. G. (ed.) (1984) *The Research Process in Educational Settings*, Lewes, Falmer.

Burgess, R. G. (ed.) (1986) *Key Variables in Social Investigation*, London, Routledge and Kegan Paul.

Burgess, R.G. (1989) *The Ethics of Educational Research*, Lewes, Falmer.

Burney, E. (1979) *J.P., Magistrate, Court and Community*, London, Hutchinson.

Campbell, D. (1957) 'Factors relevant to the validity of experiments in social settings', *Psychological Bulletin*, **54**, 4, pp. 297–312.

Campbell, D. and Stanley, J. (1963) 'Experimental and quasi-experimental designs for research on teaching', in N. Gage (ed.) *Handbook of Research on Teaching*, Chicago, Rand McNally.

Carr, W. (1987) 'What is an educational practice?', *Journal of Philosophy of Education*, **21**, 2, pp. 163–75.

Carr, W. and Kemmis, S. (1986) *Becoming Critical: education, knowledge and action research*, Lewes, Falmer.

Cherrington, R., Tomlinson, D. and Watt, P. (1987) 'Pinch and Clark's patter merchanting and the crisis of sociology', *Sociology*, **21**, 1, pp. 275–80.

Christie, R and Jahoda, M. (eds) (1954) *Studies in the Scope and Method of 'The Authoritarian Personality'*, Glencoe, Free Press.

Cicourel A. and Kitsuse J. (1973) *The Educational Decision-Makers*, Indianapolis, Bobbs-Merrill.

Clifford, J. (1983) 'On ethnographic authority', *Representations*, **1**, 2, pp. 118–44.

Clifford, J. (1988) *The Predicament of Culture*, Cambridge, Harvard University Press.

Clifford, J. and Marcus, G. (1986) *Writing Culture: the poetics and politics of ethnography*, Berkeley, University of California Press.

Cohen, A. P. (ed.) (1982) *Belonging: identity and social organisation in British rural cultures*, Manchester, Manchester University Press.

Cohen, A. P. (ed.) (1986) *Symbolising Boundaries: identity and diversity in British cultures*, Manchester, Manchester University Press.

Cohen, S. (1980) 'Ethnography without tears', *Urban Life*, **9**, 1, pp. 25–8.

Cole, J. (1977) 'Anthropology comes part way home', *Annual Review of Anthropology*, **6**, pp. 349–78.

Collins, H. M. (1975) 'The seven sexes: a study of the sociology of a phenomenon, or the replication of experiments in physics', *Sociology*, 9, pp. 205–24. Reprinted in B. Barnes and D. Edge (eds) *Science in Context*, Milton Keynes, Open University Press.

Cook, T. D. and Campbell, D. (1979) *Quasi-Experimentation*, Chicago, Rand McNally.

Crapanzano, V. (1980) *Tuhami: portrait of a Moroccan*, Chicago, University of Chicago Press.

Cressey, D. (1950) 'The criminal violation of financial trust', *American Sociological Review*, **15**, pp. 738–43.

Cressey, D. (1953) *Other People's Money*, Glencoe, Ill., Free Press.

Cressey, P. (1932) *The Taxi Dance Hall*, Chicago, University of Chicago Press.

Dalton, M. (1959) *Men Who Manage*, New York, Wiley.

Danneker, D. and Kasen, J. (1981) 'Anonymous exchanges: CB and the experience of sex typing', *Urban Life*, **10**, 3, pp. 265–87.

Darnell, R. (1974) *Readings in the History of Anthropology*, New York, Harper and Row.

Darnell, R. (1977) 'History of anthropology in historical perspective', *Annual Review of Anthropology*, **6**, pp. 399–417.

Davis, F. (1961) 'Comment', *Social Problems*, **8**, pp. 364–5.

Denzin, N. (1978) (2nd edition) *The Research Act in Sociology*, New York, McGraw-Hill.

Ditton, J. (1977) *Part-time Crime: an ethnography of fiddling and pilferage*, London, Macmillan.

Dobbert M. (1984) *Ethnographic Research: theory and application for modern schools and societies*, New York, Praeger.

Dollard, J. (1971) *Criteria for the Life History*, Freeport, New York, Libraries Press.

Douglas, J. (1976) *Investigative Social Research*, Beverly Hills, Sage.

Doyle, W. (1977) 'Learning the classroom environment', *Journal of Teacher Education*, **28**, No. 6, pp. 51–5.

Dunning, E., Murphy, P. and Williams, J. (1988) *The Roots of Football Hooliganism*, London, Routledge and Kegan Paul.

Eagleton, T. (1983) *Literary Theory: an introduction*, Oxford, Blackwell.

Edmondson, R. (1984) *Rhetoric in Sociology*, London, Macmillan.

Emmett, I. (1964) *A North Wales Village: a social anthropological study*, London, Routledge and Kegan Paul.

Engels, F. (1892) *The Condition of the Working Class in England*, London, Allen and Unwin.

Erikson, K. (1967) 'A comment on disguised observation', *Social Problems*, **14**, pp. 266–73.

Evans, J. (1983) 'Criteria of validity in social research: exploring the relationship between ethnographic and quantitative approaches', in M. Hammersley (ed.) *The Ethnography of Schooling: methodological issues*, Driffield, Nafferton.

Fears, D. (1977) 'Communication in English juvenile courts', *Sociological Review*, **XXV**, p. 1.

Festinger, L., Riecken, H. and Schachter, S. (1956) *When Prophecy Fails*, Minneapolis, University of Minnesota Press.

Fetterman, D. (ed.) (1984) *Ethnography in Educational Evaluation*, Beverly Hills, Sage.

Fetterman, D. and Pitman, M. (eds) (1986) *Educational Evaluation: ethnography in theory, practice and politics*, Beverly Hills, Sage.

Feyerabend, P. (1975) *Against Method*, London, Verso.

Feyerabend. P. (1978) *Science in a Free Society*, London, Verso.

Fielding, N. (1981) *The National Front*, London, Routledge and Kegan Paul.

Filstead, W. (1970) *Qualitative Methodology*, Chicago, Markham.

Foster, P. (1990) 'Cases not proven: an evaluation of two studies of teacher racism', *British Educational Research Journal*, **16**, 4.

Frake, C. (1962) 'The ethnographic study of cognitive systems', in T.Gladwin and W. Sturtevant (eds) *Anthropology and Human Behavior*, Washington DC, Anthropological Society of Washington.

Frankenberg, R. (1966) *Communities in Britain*, Harmondsworth, Penguin.

Freeman, D. (1984) *Margaret Mead and Samoa*, Harmondsworth, Penguin.

French, J. and French, P. (1984) 'Gender imbalances in the primary classroom', *Educational Research*, **26**, 2, pp. 127–36.

Fuller, M. (1980) 'Black girls in a London comprehensive school', in R. Deem (ed.) *Schooling for Women's Work*, London, Routledge and Kegan Paul.

Furlong, V.J. (1976) 'Interaction sets in the classroom', in M. Stubbs and S. Delamont (eds) *Explorations in Classroom Observation*, Chichester, Wiley.

Gallaher, A. (1961) *Plainville Fifteen Years Later*, New York, Columbia University Press.

Gallaher, A. (1964) 'Plainville: the twice studied town', in Vidich, Bensman and Stein (eds).

Galton, M., Simon, B. and Croll, P. (1980) *Inside the Primary Classroom*, London, Routledge and Kegan Paul.

Geertz, C. (1973) *The Interpretation of Cultures*, New York, Basic Books.

Geertz, C. (1988) *Works and Lives: the anthropologist as author*, Stanford, Stanford University Press.

Glaser, B. and Strauss, A. (1967) *The Discovery of Grounded Theory*, Chicago, Aldine.

Goetz, J. and LeCompte, M. (1984) *Ethnography and Qualitative Design in Ethnographic Research*, Orlando, Academic Press.

Good, T.L. and Brophy, J. E. (1978) *Looking in Classrooms*, New York, Harper and Row.

Goodenough, W. (1957) 'Cultural anthropology and linguistics', *Georgetown University Monographs on Language and Linguistics*, No. 9, pp. 167–73.

Gordon, M. (1947) 'The concept of subculture and its application', *Social Forces*, **26**, pp. 40–2.

Gottschalk, L. (1945) *The Use of Personal Documents in History, Anthropology, and Sociology*, New York, Social Science Research Council.

Graham, H. (1983) 'Do her answers fit his questions? Women and the survey method', in E. Gamarnikow, D. Morgan, J. Purvis, and D. Taylorson (eds) *The Public and the Private*, London, Heinemann.

Habermas, J. (1973) *Theory and Practice*, Boston, Beacon Press. (First published in German, 1963.)

Habermas, J. (1987) *Knowledge and Human Interests*, Cambridge, Polity Press. (First published, in German, 1968.)

Hammersley, M. (1974) 'The organisation of pupil participation', *Sociological Review*, **22**, 3, pp. 355–68.

Hammersley, M. (1977) Units 9–10 'Teacher Perspectives', *E202 Schooling and Society*, Milton Keynes, Open University Press.

Hammersley, M. (1980) *A Peculiar World? Teaching and learning in an inner city school*, Unpublished PhD thesis, University of Manchester.

Hammersley, M. (1981) 'Ideology in the staffroom: a critique of false consciousness', in L. Barton and S. Walker (eds) *Schools, Teachers and Teaching*, Lewes, Falmer.

Hammersley, M. (1984) 'The researcher exposed: a natural history', in Burgess, R. G. (ed.).

Hammersley, M. (1985) 'From ethnography to theory', *Sociology*, **19**, 2, pp. 244–59.

Hammersley, M, (1987a) 'Some notes on the terms ''validity'' and ''reliability''', *British Educational Research Journal*, **13**, 1, pp. 73–81.

Hammersley, M. (1987b) 'Ethnography and the cumulative development of theory', *British Educational Research Journal*, **13**, 3, pp. 283–96.

Hammersley, M. (1989a) *The Dilemma of Qualitative Method: Herbert Blumer and the Chicago tradition*, London, Routledge.

Hammersley, M. (1989b) 'The relevance of ethnography', unpublished.

Hammersley, M. (1990a) 'An assessment of two studies of gender imbalance in primary classrooms', *British Educational Research Journal*, **16**, 2, pp. 125–43

Hammersley, M. (1990b) 'A myth of a myth? an assessment of two studies of option choice in secondary schools', *British Journal of Sociology*, **41**, 2.

Hammersley, M. (1990c) 'What's wrong with ethnography? The myth of theoretical description', *Sociology*, **24**, 4, pp. 597–615.

Hammersley, M. (1990d) *Classroom Ethnography: substantive and methodological essays*, Milton Keynes, Open University Press.

Hammersley, M. (1990e) 'On feminist methodology', unpublished.

Hammersley, M. (1990f) 'Critical Theory as a model for social research', unpublished.

Hammersley, M. (1991) 'A note on Campbell's distinction between internal and external validity', *Quality and Quantity*, forthcoming.

Hammersley, M. and Atkinson, P. (1983) *Ethnography: principles in practice*, London, Tavistock.

Hammersley, M. and Scarth, J. (1990) 'On teachers as researchers', unpublished.

Hammersley, M. and Turner, G. (1980) 'Conformist pupils?', in P. Woods (ed.) *Pupil Strategies*, London, Croom Helm.

Hannerz, U. (1969) *Soulside: inquiries into ghetto culture and community*, New York, Columbia University Press.

Harding, S. (1987) (ed.) *Feminism and Methodology*, Bloomington, Indiana University Press.

Hargreaves, A. (1978) 'The significance of classroom coping strategies', in L. Barton and R. Meighan (eds) *Sociological Interpretations of Schooling and Classrooms*, Driffield, Nafferton.

Hargreaves, A. (1984) Unit 22, Marxism and Relative Autonomy, Open University course *E205, Conflict and Change in Education*, Milton Keynes, Open University Press.

Hargreaves, D. H. (1967) *Social Relations in a Secondary School*, London, Routledge and Kegan Paul.

Hargreaves, D. H. (1972) *Interpersonal Relations and Education*, London, Routledge and Kegan Paul.

Hargreaves, D. H. (1977) 'The process of typification in the classroom', *British Journal of Educational Psychology*, **47**, pp. 27–84.

Hargreaves, D. H. (1978) 'Whatever happened to Symbolic Interactionism?', in L. Barton and R. Meighan (eds) *Sociological Interpretations of Schooling and Classrooms*, Driffield, Nafferton.

Hargreaves, D. H. (1980) 'The occupational culture of teachers', in P. Woods, (ed.) *Teacher Strategies*, London, Croom Helm.

Hargreaves, D. H., Hester, S. and Mellor, F. (1975) *Deviance in Classrooms*, London, Routledge and Kegan Paul.

Harré, R. and Secord P. (1973) *The Explanation of Social Behaviour*, Oxford, Blackwell.

Hart, H. and Honoré, T. (1985) (2nd edition) *Causation and the Law*, Oxford, Oxford University Press.

Harvey, L. (1987) *Myths of the Chicago School*, Aldershot, Gower.

Hickrod, L. J. H. and Schmitt, R. L. (1982) 'A naturalistic study of interaction and frame: the pet as a "family member"', *Urban Life*, **11**, 1, pp. 55–78.

Hirst, P. H. (1971) 'What is teaching', *Journal of Curriculum Studies*, **3**, 1, pp. 9–10.

Hitchcock, G. (1983) 'Fieldwork as practical activity', in M. Hammersley (ed.) *The Ethnography of Schooling*, Driffield, Nafferton.

Homan, R. (1978) 'Interpersonal communication in pentecostal meetings', *Sociological Review*, **26**, pp. 499–518.

Honigmann, J. (1970) 'Fieldwork in two northern Canadian communities', in M. Freilich (ed.) *Marginal Natives: anthropologists at work*, New York, Harper and Row.

Ingleby, D. (1976) 'The psychology of child psychology', in R. Dale *et al.* (eds) *Schooling and Capitalism*, London, Routledge and Kegan Paul.

Jackson, P. (1968) *Life in Classrooms*, New York, Holt, Rinehart and Winston.

Janowitz, M. (1971) *Sociological Methods and Social Policy*, New York, General Learning Press.

Jay, M. (1984) *Marxism and Totality*, Cambridge, Polity.

Jenkins, D. (n.d.) 'An adversary's account of Safari's ethics of case study', in C. Richards (eds) *Power and the Curriculum*, Driffield, Nafferton.

Johnson, J. (1975) *Doing Field Research*, New York, The Free Press.

Kaberry, P. (1957) 'Malinowski's contribution to field–work methods and the writing of ethnography', in R. Firth (ed.) *Man and Culture*, London, Routledge and Kegan Paul.

Katzer, J., Cook, K. and Crouch, W. (1978) *Evaluating Information: a guide for users of social science research*, Reading, Mass., Addison-Wesley.

Keat, R. and Urry, J. (1975) *Social Theory as Science*, London, Routledge and Kegan Paul.

Kelly, A. (1985) 'Action research: what is it and what can it do?', in R. Burgess (ed.) *Issues in Educational Research*, Lewes, Falmer.

Kirk, J. and Miller, M. (1986) *Reliability and Validity in Qualitative Research*, Beverly Hills, Sage.

Klockars, C. (1974) *The Professional Fence*, London, Tavistock.

Kolakowski, L. (1978) *Main Currents of Marxism,* vol. III, Oxford, Oxford University Press.

Krieger, S. (1983) *The Mirror Dance*, Philadelphia, Temple University Press.

Kuhn, T. (1970) (2nd edition) *The Structure of Scientific Revolutions*, Chicago, University of Chicago Press.

Lacey, C. (1970) *Hightown Grammar*, Manchester, Manchester University Press.

Lacey, C. (1974) 'Destreaming in a "pressured" academic environment', in J. Eggleston (ed.) *Contemporary Research in the Sociology of Education*, London, Methuen.

Larmore, C. (1987) *Patterns of Moral Complexity*, Cambridge, Cambridge University Press.

LeCompte, M. and Goetz, J. (1982) 'Problems of reliability and validity in ethnographic research', *Review of Educational Research*, **52**, 1, pp. 31–60.

Lehman, T. and Young, T. (1974) 'From conflict theory to conflict methodology', *Sociological Inquiry*, **44**, pp. 15–28.

Leiter, K. (1974) 'Ad hocing in the schools' in A. V. Cicourel *et al.* (eds) *Language Use and School Performance*, New York, Academic Press.

Lejeune, R. (1977) 'The management of a mugging', *Urban Life*, **6**, pp. 123–48.

Lejeune, R. (1980) 'A note on "The management of a mugging"', *Urban Life*, **9**, 1, pp. 113–9.

Lessnoff, M. (1974) *The Structure of Social Science*, London, Allen and Unwin.

Lever, J. (1981) 'Multiple methods of data collection', *Urban Life*, **10**, 2, pp. 199–213.

Lewis, O. (1961) *The Children of Sanchez*, New York, Vintage.

Lewis, O. (1964) *Pedro Martinez: a Mexican peasant and his family*, London, Secker and Warburg.

Lewis, O. (1970) *A Death in the Sanchez Family*, London, Secker and Warburg.

Liazos, A. (1972) 'The poverty of the sociology of deviance: nuts, sluts and perverts', *Social Problems*, **20**, pp. 103–20.

Lichtheim, G. (1970) *Lukacs*, London, Fontana/Collins.

Lincoln, Y. and Guba, E. (1985) *Naturalistic Inquiry*, Beverly Hills, Sage.

Lindblom, C. and Cohen, D. (1979) *Usable Knowledge: social science and social problem solving*, New Haven, Yale University Press.

Lindesmith, A. (1937) *The Nature of Opiate Addiction*, Chicago, University of Chicago Libraries.

Lindesmith, A. (1968) *Addiction and Opiates*, Chicago, Aldine.

Lobkowicz, N. (1967) *Theory and Practice*, Notre Dame, University of Notre Dame Press.

Lofland, J. (1961) 'Reply to Davis', *Social Problems*, **8**, pp. 365–7.

Lofland, J. (1972) *Analyzing Social Settings*, Belmont, California, Wadsworth.

Lofland, J. (1974) 'Styles of reporting qualitative field research', *American Sociologist*, **9**, pp. 101–11.

Lofland, J. and Lejeune, R. (1960) 'Initial interaction of newcomers in Alcoholics Anonymous', *Social Problems*, **8**, pp. 102–11.

Lofland, J. and L. (1983) (2nd edition) *Analyzing Social Settings*, Belmont, California, Wadsworth.

Lortie, D. (1975) *Schoolteacher*, Chicago, University of Chicago Press.

Lukacs, G. (1971) *History and Class Consciousness*, London, Merlin.

Lundman, R. and McFarlane, P. (1976) 'Conflict methodology: an introduction and preliminary assessment', *Sociological Quarterly*, **17**, pp. 503–12.

Lyman, S.M. and Scott, M.B. (1970) *A Sociology of the Absurd*, New York, Appleton Crofts.

Lynd, R. S. and Lynd, H. M. (1929) *Middletown: a study in contemporary American culture*, New York, Harcourt Brace.

Lynd, R. S. and Lynd, H. M. (1937) *Middletown in Transition: a study in cultural conflicts*, New York, Harcourt Brace.

van Maanen, J. (1988) *Tales of the Field*, Chicago, University of Chicago Press.

McCall, G. and Simmons, J. (1969) *Issues in Participant Observation*, Reading, Mass. Addison–Wesley.

McCarthy, T. (1978) *The Critical Theory of Jurgen Habermas*, London, Hutchinson.

MacDonald, B. (1974) 'Evaluation and the control of education', in B. MacDonald and R. Walker (eds) *Safari: Innovation, Evaluation, Research and the Problem of Control*, Norwich, Centre for Applied Research in Education, University of East Anglia.

McKinney, D. W. (1973) *The Authoritarian Personality Studies: an inquiry into the failure of social science research to produce demonstrable knowledge,* The Hague, Mouton.

McNall, S. and Johnson, J. (1975) 'The new conservatives: ethnomethodologists, phenomenologists and symbolic interactionists', *Insurgent Sociologist*, **V**, IV, pp. 49–65.

Madge, J. (1963) *The Origins of Scientific Sociology*, London, Tavistock.

Marcus, G. and Cushman, D. (1982) 'Ethnographies as texts', *Annual Review of Anthropology*, **11**, pp. 25–69.

Marcus, G. and Fischer, M. (1986) *Anthropology as Cultural Critique*, Chicago, University of Chicago Press.

Mars, G. (1974) 'Dock pilferage', in P. Rock and M. McIntosh (eds) *Deviance and Social Control*, London, Tavistock.

Marsh, P., Rosser, E. and Harré, R. (1978) *The Rules of Disorder*, London, Routledge and Kegan Paul.

Marx, K. (1845) 'Theses on Feuerbach', in K. Marx and F. Engels, *Selected Works*, London, Lawrence and Wishart, 1968.

Matza, D. (1964) *Delinquency and Drift*, New York, Wiley.

Matza, D. (1969) *Becoming Deviant*, Englewood Cliffs, Prentice Hall.

Mayhew, H. (1861–2) *London Labour and the London Poor*, London, Cass.

Mayhew, H. (1971) *The Unknown Mayhew*, edited by E. P. Thompson and E. Yeo, London, Merlin Press.

Merton, R. K. (1957) *Social Theory and Social Structure*, New York, Free Press.

Merton, R. K. and Lazarsfeld, P. F. (eds) (1950) *Continuities in Social Research: studies in the scope and method of 'The American Soldier'*, Glencoe, Free Press.

Mies, M. (1983) 'Towards a methodology for feminist research', in G. Bowles and R.Klein (eds) *Theories of Women's Studies*, London, Routledge.

Miles, M. and Huberman (1984) *Qualitative Data Analysis*, Beverly Hills, Sage.

Miller, A. (1986) *The Obedience Experiments: a case study of controversy in social science*, New York, Praeger

Nash, R. (1973) *Classrooms Observed*, London, Routledge and Kegan Paul.

Newton-Smith, W. H. (1981) *The Rationality of Science*, London, Routledge and Kegan Paul.

Newton-Smith, W. H. (1990) 'Realism', in R. Colby, G. Cantor, J. Christie and M. Hodge (eds) *Companion to the History of Modern Science*, London, Routledge.

Noblitt, G. and Hare, R. (1988) *Meta-Ethnography: synthesizing qualitative studies*, Newbury Park, Sage.

Norris, C. (1982) *Deconstruction: theory and practice*, London, Routledge.

Oakes, G. (1988) *Weber and Rickert: concept formation in the social sciences*, Cambridge, Mass., MIT Press.

Ochs, E. (1979) 'Transcriptions as theory' in E. Ochs, (ed.) *Developmental Pragmatics*, New York, Academic Press.

Owens, R. (1982) 'Methodological rigor in naturalistic inquiry', *Educational Administration Quarterly*, **18**, 2, pp. 1–21.

Parker, H., Casburn, M. and Turnbull, D. (1981) *Receiving Juvenile Justice*, Oxford, Blackwell.

Passmore, J. (1978) *Science and its Critics*, London, Duckworth.

Payne, G., Dingwall, R., Payne, J. and Carter, M. (1981) *Sociology and Social Research*, London, Routledge and Kegan Paul.

Pinch, T. and Clark, C. (1986) 'The hard sell: "patter merchanting" and the strategic (re)production of economic reasoning in the sales routines of market pitchers', *Sociology*, **20**, 2, pp. 169–91.

Pinch, T. and Clark, C. (1987) 'On misunderstanding the hard sell', *Sociology*, **21**, 2, pp. 281–6.

Platt, J. (1971) *Social Research in Bethnal Green: an evaluation of the work of the Institute for Community Study*, London, Macmillan.

Plummer, K. (1983) *Documents of Life*, London, Allen and Unwin.

Polanyi, M. (1968) 'The republic of science', in E. Shils (ed.) *Criteria for Scientific Development*, Cambridge, Mass., MIT Press.

Pollard, A. (1984) 'Coping strategies and the multiplication of differentiation in infant classrooms', *British Educational Research Journal*, **10**, 1, pp. 33–48.

Pollert, A. (1981) *Girls, Wives, Factory Lives*, London, Macmillan.

Popper, K. R. (1959) *The Logic of Scientific Discovery*, London, Routledge and Kegan Paul.

Posner, J. (1980) 'On sociology chic: notes on a possible direction for symbolic interactionism', *Urban Life*, **9**, 1, pp. 103–12.

Pratt, M. L. (1986) 'Fieldwork in common places', in Clifford and Marcus (eds).

Punch, M. (1979) *Policing the Inner City: a study of Amsterdam's Warmoesstraat*, London, Macmillan.

Quine, W. G. (1974) 'Polarised cultures in comprehensive schools', *Research in Education*, **12**, pp. 9–25.

Radin, P. (1926) *Crashing Thunder: the autobiography of a Winnebago Indian*, New York, D. Appleton.

Rainwater, L. and Pitman, D. (1967) 'Ethical problems in studying a politically sensitive and deviant community', *Social Problems*, **14**, pp. 357–66.

Reynolds, P. (1982) *Ethics and Social Research*, Englewood Cliffs, Prentice Hall.

Richards, I. A. (1943) *How to Read a Page*, London, Routledge and Kegan Paul.

Rist, R. (1970) 'Student social class and teacher expectations', *Harvard Educational Review*, **40**, 3, pp. 411–51

Rist, R. (1973) *The Urban School*, Cambridge, Mass., MIT Press.

Rist, R. (1977) 'On the relations among educational research paradigms: from disdain to detente', *Anthropology and Educational Quarterly*, **VIII**, 2, pp. 42–49.

Robinson, W. (1951) 'The logical structure of analytic induction', *American Sociological Review*, **16**, 6, pp. 812–18.

Rock, P. (1973) *Making People Pay*, London, Routledge.

Rose, A. (ed.) (1962) *Human Behavior and Social Processes*, London, Routledge and Kegan Paul.

Rose, G. (1982) *Deciphering Sociological Research*, London, Macmillan.

Rosenthal, R. and Jacobson, L. (1968) *Pygmalion in the Classroom*, New York, Holt, Rinehart and Winston.

Roth, J. (1962) 'Comments on secret observation', *Social Problems*, **9**, pp. 283–4.

Rowe, J. H. (1965) 'The renaissance foundations of anthropology', *American Anthropologist*, **67**, pp. 1–20.

Roy, D. (1952) 'Quota restriction and goldbricking in a machine shop', *American Journal of Sociology*, **57**, pp. 427–42.

Roy, D. (1955) 'Efficiency and the fix', *American Journal of Sociology*, **60**, pp. 255–66.

Rynkiewich, M. and Spradley, J. (eds) (1976) *Ethics and Anthropology: dilemmas in fieldwork*, New York, Wiley.

Sagarin, E. (1980) 'Commentary on "Sociology chic"', *Urban Life*, **9**, 1, pp. 12–14.

Scarth, J. (1987) 'Teacher strategies: a review and critique', *British Journal of Sociology of Education*, **8**, 3, pp. 245–62.

Schatzman, L. and Strauss, A. (1973) *Field Research: strategies for a natural sociology*, Englewood Cliffs, Prentice Hall.

Schegloff, E. (1968) 'Sequencing in conversational openings', *American Anthropologist*, **70**, pp. 1075–95.

Schon, D. (1983) *The Reflective Practitioner*, London, Temple Smith.

Schon, D. (1987) *Educating the Reflective Practitioner*, San Francisco, Jossey–Bass.

Schwab, J. (1978) *Science, Curriculum and Liberal Education*, Chicago, University of Chicago Press.

Scott, J. (1990) *A Matter of Record: documentary sources in social research*, Cambridge, Polity Press.

Sharp, R. and Green, A. (1975) *Education and Social Control*, London, Routledge and Kegan Paul.

Sharrock, W. and Anderson, R. (1986) *The Ethnomethodologists*, Chichester, Horwood/London, Tavistock.

Shaw, C. (1930) *The Jack Roller*, Chicago, University of Chicago Press (reprinted 1966 with an introduction by H. S. Becker).

Shostak, M. (1981) *Nisa: the life and words of a !Kung Woman*, Cambridge, Mass., Harvard University Press.

Siegel, H. (1987) *Relativism Refuted*, Dordrecht, Reidel.

Siegel, H. (1989) 'Farewell to Feyerabend', *Inquiry*, 32, pp. 343–69.

Smart, C. (1984) *The Ties that Bind*, London, Routledge and Kegan Paul.

Smith, D. (1978) '"K is mentally ill": The anatomy of a factual account', *Sociology*, **12**, 1, pp. 23–53.

Smith, J. K. and Heshusius, L. (1986) 'Closing down the conversation: the end of the quantitative-qualitative debate among educational inquirers' *Educational Researcher*, **15**, 1, pp. 4–12.

Spender, D. (1982) *Invisible Women*, London, Writers and Readers Publishing Cooperative Society and Chameleon Editorial Group.

Sperber, D. and Wilson, D. (1986) *Relevance: communication and cognition*, Oxford, Blackwell.

Spradley, J. P. (1979) *The Ethnographic Interview*, New York, Holt, Rinehart and Winston.

Stacey, M. (1960) *Tradition and Change: a study of Banbury*, Oxford, Oxford University Press.

Stacey, M., Batstone, E., Bell, C. and Murcott, A. (1975) *Power, Persistence and Change*, London, Routledge and Kegan Paul.

Stanworth, M. (1981) *Gender and Schooling: a study of sexual divisions in the classroom*, London, Women's Research and Resources Group.

Stebbins, R. (1975) *Teachers and Meaning*, New York, Brill.

Stebbins, R. (1982) 'Amateur and professional astronomers: a study of their interrelationships', *Urban Life*, **10**, 4, pp. 433–54.

Stenhouse, L. (1975) *An Introduction to Curriculum Research and Development*, London, Heinemann.

Stern, P. (1979) *Evaluating Social Science Research*, New York, Oxford University Press.

Strong, P. M. (1979) *The Ceremonial Order of the Clinic: parents, doctors and medical bureaucracies*, London, Routledge and Kegan Paul.

Strong, P. M. (1988) 'Qualitative sociology in the UK', *Qualitative Sociology*, **11**, 1 and 2, pp. 13–28.

Sutherland, E. (1956) *The Sutherland Papers*, (edited by Cohen, A., Lindesmith, A. and Schuessler, K.), Bloomington, Indiana University Press.

Tiles, M. (1988) 'Science and the world', in G. Parkinson (ed.) *An Encyclopedia of Philosophy*, London, Routledge.

Tocqueville, A. (1966) *Democracy in America*, two volumes, New York, Harper and Row. (First published, in French, in 1835 and 1840.)

Tripodi, T., Fellin, P. and Meyer, H. (1969) *The Assessment of Social Research: Guidelines for the use of social research in social work and social science*, Itasca, Illinois, Peacock.

Vidich, A. and Bensman, J. (1958) *Small Town in a Mass Society*, Princeton, Princeton University Press.

Vidich, A. and Bensman, J. (1964) 'The Springdale Case: academic bureaucrats and sensitive townspeople', in Vidich, Bensman and Stein (eds).

Vidich, A., Bensman, J. and Stein, M. (eds) (1964) *Reflections on Community Studies*, New York, Wiley.

Walker, D. (1980) *The Oxford Companion to Law*, Oxford, Clarendon Press.

Walker, R. (1974) 'The conduct of educational case study: ethics, theory and procedures', in B. MacDonald and R. Walker (eds) *Safari: Innovation, Evaluation, Research and the Problem of Control*, Norwich, Centre for Applied Research in Education, University of East Anglia.

Waller, W. (1967) *The Sociology of Teaching*, New York, Wiley. (First published in 1932.)

Warner, W.L. (1963) *Yankee City*, New Haven, Yale University Press.

Wax, M. (1972) 'Tenting with Malinowski', *American Sociological Review*, **37**, 1, pp. 1–13.

Wax, R. (1971) *Doing Fieldwork: warnings and advice*, Chicago, University of Chicago Press.

Weber, M. (1958) 'Politics as a vocation', in H. Gerth and C. Wright Mills (eds) *From Max Weber*, London, Routledge.

West, W. G. (1984) 'Phenomenon and form in interactionist and neo-marxist qualitative educational research', in L. Barton and S. Walker (eds) *Social Crisis and Educational Research*, London, Croom Helm.

Westley, W. (1970) *Violence and the Police*, Cambridge, Mass., MIT Press.

Whyte, W. F. (1981) (3rd edition), *Street Corner Society: the social structure of an Italian slum*, Chicago, University of Chicago Press.

Wieder, D. L. (1974) *Language and Social Reality*, The Hague, Mouton.

Williams, W. M. (1956) *The Sociology of an English Village: Gosforth*, London, Routledge and Kegan Paul.

Willis, P. (1977) *Learning to Labour*, Farnborough, Saxon House.

Winch, P. (1964) 'Understanding a primitive society', *American Philosophical Quarterly*, **1**, pp. 304–24.

Wolcott, H. (1975) 'Criteria for an ethnographic approach to research in schools', *Human Organization*, **34**, pp. 111–127.

Wolcott, H. (1982) 'Mirrors, models, and monitors: educator adaptations of the ethnographic innovation', in G. Spindler (ed.) *Doing the Ethnography of Schooling: educational anthropology in action*, New York, Holt, Rinehart and Winston.

Woods, P. (1977) 'Stages in interpretive research', *Research Intelligence*, **3**, 1, pp. 17–18.

Woods, P. (1979a) *The Divided School*, London, Routledge and Kegan Paul.

Woods, P. (1979b) 'How teachers decide pupils' subject choices', in J. Eggleston (ed.) *Teacher Decision-Making in the Classroom*, London, Routledge and Kegan Paul.

Znaniecki, F. (1934) *The Method of Sociology*, New York, Farrer and Rinehart.

Zorbaugh, H. (1929) *The Gold Coast and the Slum*, Chicago, University of Chicago Press.

SUBJECT INDEX

AUTHOR INDEX